To Mehn

[signature]

TALK TO ME,
MOM AND DAD

Electronic and soft-cover print versions
published by the Wellness Institute,Inc.
1007 Whitney Avenue, Gretna, LA 70056
May 1, 2000.

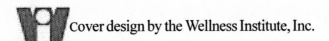Cover design by the Wellness Institute, Inc.

SelfHelpBooks.com is a division of the
Wellness Institute, Inc.
Gretna, LA 70056

ISBN: 1-58741-072-9
Printed in the United States of America

SELFHELPBOOKS.COM

SelfHelpBooks.com is the Internet's largest publisher/bookseller exclusively selling self-help books. It is a site where anyone can find the right self-help book in just minutes. Books are available for immediate download or in a print version that can be promptly shipped and received within days.

New self-help books are reviewed and added on a continual basis and out-of-print books are republished so that visitors can have the widest possible selection of good self-help books.

TALK TO ME, MOM AND DAD

By Anita Remig, Ed.D.

ABOUT THE AUTHOR

Dr. Anita Remig is a psychologist who has been in private practice for twenty years, working with children, adolescents and families. Her specialty areas include Communication Training and Solution-Focused Therapy. Children and teenagers with problems such as Attention-Deficit/Hyperactive Disorder, Motivation Deficits, Developmental Disorders, and Oppositional Defiance require help getting their needs met within the family.

Dr. Remig uses principles discussed in her book to facilitate talking and growing for all family members. She does psychological evaluations for the above-mentioned emotional and cognitive issues.

Teaching at the college level has been a part-time focus of Dr. Remig's career. As well, she travels throughout the United States giving seminars to teaching and counseling professionals.

New Hampshire has been her home for the last ten years where she lives with her husband, two sons and a daughter.

Table of Contents

Introduction

SECTION I BUILDING BLOCKS OF LANGUAGE

Chapter 1 Motivation, Thinking, Feeling and Talking

Chapter 2 Keep Talking, Mom and Dad!

Chapter 3 The First Word

Chapter 4 Language Takes Off

Chapter 5 Teach Me How to Talk to You, Baby

Chapter 6 People Talk

Chapter 7 Getting Ready For School?

SECTION II FAMILY BUILDING

Chapter 8 Family Language

Chapter 9 Angry Talk

Chapter 10 Guide Me and Discipline Me, Mom and Dad

Chapter 11 Pitfalls in Children's Verbal Performance

Chapter 12 Moving Toward the Teenage Years

SECTION III BUILDING BLOCKS

Chapter 13 Parents Give to Get

Chapter 14 Listen to Me, Mom and Dad

Chapter 15 Girls' Talk, Boys' Talk

Chapter 16 Single Parent's Talk

Chapter 17 Talking and Biking

Publisher's Note

INTRODUCTION

"Once a human being has arrived on this earth, communication is the largest single factor determining what kinds of relationships he makes with others and what happens to him in the world about him."

-Virginia Satir

Tina dreaded the idea of going to kindergarten, and when she had to get on the bus she fell apart. She screamed and cried but, nonetheless, was pushed aboard by her parents. When she arrived at school she was crying and upset. She was ignored by her teacher for the most part that first day, but when she came to school crying, distraught and frightened every day for many weeks and eventually months, her teacher routinely put her in the closet to stand there for sometimes several hours. Tina never told any one at home that she was put in the supply closet at school; she never told anyone at school that she was pushed onto the bus by her parents. She resisted going to school for most of her kindergarten year while her mother dutifully pushed her onto the bus each morning. No one at home or school ever asked Tina what was wrong. Her parents did not say, "What is the problem?" They did not talk to her. They did not communicate. Neither did the teacher nor anyone else at the school. No one ever said, "Let us talk about these feelings you have. Let us get to the bottom of what is bothering you." And yet, all the while, five-year-old year Tina longed to say, "Talk to me, Mom and Dad."

As an adult Tina now understands what went wrong with her first school experience. She needed caring and empathic communication; she needed an adult to talk to her. She needed someone, whether mother, grandmother, father, teacher, psychologist, principal or anyone to discuss her troubles and her fears with, as all children do.

When Tina was a child she wanted someone to talk to her. She wanted to understand her feelings, to work out problems with her sisters, parents, and friends. She felt alone and did not know how to reach out and get someone to help her open up. She longed to understand people; she knew that the feelings she experienced were not what they should be. She was confused, and knew she needed support. She wanted to listen to a sensitive adult, and she desperately wanted someone to listen to her. When she tried to talk to the adults in her life, they had no time for her and now she realizes it was not just a time problem. They did not know how to communicate with her, nor did they know how to communicate with one another.

The "talk to me" need does not go away as children grow into adolescence and adulthood. All people, young and old, need talking that is intimate, caring, and empathic. As an adult, Tina is still looking for people with whom she can talk. I am deeply touched by people like Tina who come from troubled beginnings, yet yearn to get the caring communication from other people. Language and communication can bring us from silent despair and confusion out into the light where it is safe and healing to talk and share. I believe in the talking process as a method of healing the self and past problems, and of solving difficulties between people in families, in groups, in communities, and even among nations. There is no other way but to rely on calm, rational, heartfelt communication to get problems solved.

I am a psychologist and I practice psychotherapy with children, adults and families. All of the people you will encounter in this book, including Tina and her children, are real people. In order to protect their privacy, I have changed names, salient facts, and some circumstances that would reveal their identity. I believe that real people's thoughts, feelings, and talking would provide far richer and more interesting stories than any I could make up.

After I finished my doctoral program, I married and had three children. I spend many hours a week now listening to people, and I find this work to be very satisfying. Likewise at home, I spend time talking with my family and making an effort to support them and communicate with them.

This brings us to the purpose of this book: Should children be able to say "Talk to me, Mom and Dad," and why? We hear from all the experts that healthy family communication is good. We are told that it is good to talk to our children and spouses. We are told that language plays a powerful role in creating relationships and solving human problems. But even well-meaning adults are unable sometimes to use language that is helpful, supportive, and meaningful to children. This leads to important questions: What is the goal of our communication? What kind of language should we use to support children? Is any kind of talk healthy as long as we are conversing? What is a good balance between talking and listening? Are there preferred ways of talking to children when we are disciplining them? What is the difference between explaining and criticizing? These and other questions are raised in this book. The goal of this book is to explain the importance of language and communication in family life.

All children need to be given basic physical care: food, shelter, and clothing. That is something we can all agree on. But what is hard to understand, and even harder to accomplish, is satisfactory parent-child relationships based on effective communication. Unlike animals, we can use language to express ourselves and understand other people. People, on the whole, are just beginning to use this distinctly human ability fully. We are just beginning to grasp the power of the word and how to use it to build bridges instead of create barriers.

My method in this book is to examine communication between people and show how parents can foster it from the early days of a child's life. The importance of effective communication among people and healthy parent-child communication cannot be over-emphasized. The distinctly human ability to converse forms the foundation for all of society and all of culture. If we could not convey information to each other, our world would collapse. To the extent that we convey information effectively, society functions effectively. Language is the most powerful tool human beings can use to communicate with each other. All human relationships involve some type of language whether it is spoken, written, or signed. Language is important for building relationships, transmitting information, and learning skills. Thus, language proficiency assists with our mental, emotional, social, and physical development. Our capacity to use language to communicate scientific and humanitarian ideas plays a crucial role in the progress of civilization, and individuals who use language well are typically the most successful and competent. Thus, parents who teach their children effective language skills produce children who thrive mentally, socially, and emotionally. We need to teach our children sensitive and intelligent communication so that we can strengthen our relationships with them and prepare them for their place in the world. People who listen well and express themselves clearly are successful in school and are likely to get satisfying jobs and to earn a comfortable living. I look at communication as a four-step process; the steps are (1) motivation, which leads to (2) thinking, which then arouses (3) feeling, which prompts us to (4) talk, and express our motivations and thinking. After we talk, the whole process begins again as our own speech and other people's ideas set the cycle in motion once more. Motivation stirs inside, our thoughts are formed, our feelings swell, and words are produced. The words do not leave our mouths until they are edited and changed; then we finally speak. So talking is not just "words from the mouth." Talking includes our will, mental capacity, emotions, and editing.

Language learning begins before birth. The fetus in the womb can hear after five months gestation, and the sounds and voices he hears help shape his readiness to hear and listen. After birth, playful and routine talk between parents and children influence the quality of the children's communication. Language is the most complicated system of signs and symbols people can learn, and children have gained basic understanding of the structure of sentences (syntax) by the time they are three years old!

In the first section of this book, we will look at how parents play a critical role in fostering language learning by the way they communicate with their child from infancy onward. We will explore the richness and variety of language that parents and teachers can use in talking to children. We will take a peek at how Mom and Dad can use reading time with children to promote thinking as well as communication. When an adult is familiar with the intellectual challenges his or her language can provide for children, talking and reading get lively!

The middle section of this book describes language styles that parents use with children at home. Parents discuss and arrange important life tasks including jobs, education, household duties, and childcare. They communicate with one another and their children in carrying out their daily routines. In trying to get life tasks accomplished, sometimes adults are not aware of the ways their language affects children. There are aspects of talk that make language learning and communication difficult, and the book discusses some of these problems. One problem included in this section is so-called authoritarian talk, which is not effective because it is too harsh and comes from built-up anger. The angry talk from authoritarian parents hurts children and passes on the anger. Thus, the children do not learn to communicate clearly and moderately. The opposite communication problem comes from parent talk that is inconsistent, weak, and unclear. This type of communication is common to so-called permissive parents. These parents have not straightened out their own motivation, thinking, and feeling so they can be direct and firm with their children. Children do not listen to weak and ineffectual language; they tend to disobey and act on their own impulses. Permissive language fails to set clear limits and guide the child in fair and consistent ways.

The last section of this book focuses on the impressive human capacity for using language to establish bonds. The goal of this section is to point out the pervasive role language plays in shaping relationships, supporting family and friends, and self-actualization. Our concern for clear, creative, and caring language has positive effects on our children and our own personal development.

Brown, Lyn Mikel and Gulligan, Carol *Meeting at the Crossroads:* Women's Psychology and Girl's Development. Harvard University Press, 1992.

Dobson, Keith *Handbook of Cognitive-Behavioral Therapies.* The Guilford Press, 1988.

Satir, Virginia *Peoplemaking.* Science and Behavior Books, Paolo Alto, Ca, 1972.

SECTION I
BUILDING BLOCKS OF LANGUAGE

"If survival depended solely upon the triumph of the strong then the species would perish. So the real reason for survival, the principal factor in the "struggle for existence", is the love of the adult for their young."

Maria Montessori

Chapter 1

Motivation, Thinking, Feeling and Talking

"How we think determines to a large extent, how we will succeed and enjoy life, or even survive. If our thinking is straightforward and clear, we are better equipped to reach these goals."
-Aaron T. Beck

Tina could not talk to her teacher or her classmates when she went to kindergarten. Tina did not speak much during her entire kindergarten and first grade years. And still, in spite of these ongoing problems, no one reached out to help her. The sad part of Tina's story is that it would not have taken a great effort to help her overcome her fear and end her silence. It would have taken simple know-how and a caring communicator. Let us look at how some of Tina's problems could have been solved through talking.

Adult: Do your worries about being stupid, mean and vain have anything to do with why you cry and do not talk at school?

Tina: Uh huh. I feel so bad inside that I might cry if I talk to someone at school.

Adult: That must be awful to feel so bad that you cannot talk. I want to figure out how to help you. Will you tell me more about your bad feelings?

Tina: When my father comes home I start to shake and I feel scared. Often he shouts and yells at me, at my sisters and at my mother. Sometimes he hits us. I try hard to do everything right, so then I won't get yelled at and hit. But even when I try hard I still do bad things.

Adult: Tina, we talked about mistakes before. Can good people make mistakes?

Tina: Yes, you make mistakes and you are a good person.

Adult: So how about you? I think you are a good person.

Tina: No, I am a bad person.

Adult: I know you think that, but I do not. Now, do you make mistakes?

Tina: Yes.

Adult: Does that mean you are bad? If so, then I am bad, too.

Tina: You are good. Maybe I am not bad. But why am I treated so mean by my mother and father?

Adult: You said something bigger than the biggest mountain! You said that maybe you are not bad. If you are not bad, then there is a chance you are good, right?

Tina: Yeah. But it hurts to be treated so mean at home. I am scared a lot.

Adult: Yes, it must hurt a lot. I am so sorry you are hurting. I do not like yelling and hitting. I wish I could make that stop, but I cannot. I can help you to stop yelling at yourself and hitting yourself on the inside. Does it mean that you are a bad person when the yelling and hitting come at home?

Tina: Maybe I can stop it if I am really good.

Adult: You have already tried that and it does not work because you will make mistakes just like me and everyone else. Does that mean I should get yelled at and hit? How about you?

Tina: No, for both of us.

3

The critical information about Tina is that she thinks she is bad because she makes mistakes, and is verbally and physically abused by her parents. It is her mistaken conclusion that she is bad that makes her miserable. Her belief that she is a bad person is fortified by the abuse, she punishes herself inside for being so worthless and then feels bad. Because she thinks of herself as worthless, she is unable to communicate and share her thoughts and feelings with other people at school.

The above conversation could mark a turning point in a child's life, where she begins to understand how talking to a kind, caring and compassionate adult can motivate her to seek answers to painful questions. Once a child learns that through talking she can develop a secure inner life and stays tuned to what is happening inside her, she becomes motivated to talk, to learn, to explore the world. Tina begins to learn that talking to a sympathetic adult can open up new roads for healing and growth. Communication is a potent and complex tool of the human mind.

At this point we need to look at the mind and its powerful motivating-thinking-feeling-talking capabilities that when put together, produce communication. As we know, the human mind is infinitely complex, so the following explanation is a plain and simple description of some rather detailed psychological models. I am going to describe a model of human communication. When we consider some types of mental processes we can see how the mind is set up for communication and why communication can break down at times. The first step in the four-step process of communication involves motivation.

Motivation is an internal urge or moving force that causes human beings to act. Webster's Dictionary defines a motive as an "emotion or desire acting on the will and causing it to act" that can "stimulate the faculties and increase energy and ardor" or "keep one going against one's will or desire."

Did you ever wonder what kept a jogger going on a hot, humid day or during a freezing, slippery rain? Probably his

4

motivation to exercise gets him into better physical condition, to feel better about his body and relieve tension and stress. Motivation lives and grows inside each of us and propels us to think, feel, behave and talk.

Motivation has its roots in our biological nature. We all have drives to eat, drink, seek shelter, find safety, and affiliate with other people. Abraham Maslow has described human motivation as a hierarchy where basic biological needs have to be met before a human being can go on to higher level needs. After the needs for food, shelter, and socialization are met, people are motivated by needs for esteem, which involve striving for achievement, competence and recognition. Once a person finds approval and recognition from some source, he is free to satisfy cognitive and intellectual pursuits; he can study, understand and explore. The motivation to create comes next in the hierarchy, and at this level people can create aesthetic works such as a garden, a gourmet meal or a painting. At the peak of the hierarchy, Maslow says, is self-actualization where a person seeks self-fulfillment and the realization of his potential.

After our basic physical needs are met, we have a tremendous range of possibilities in the ways we meet our higher level needs. Our motivation to belong to a social group can be satisfied by family, friends, and community organizations. Our desire to achieve can lead to an almost infinite range of activities from homemaking to glassblowing to computer technology. Our motive to learn and understand can encompass such diverse pursuits as engineering and entomology. Our choices in these matters are shaped by living in the physical world, and are refined by our experiences with family and culture.

The motivation to adopt values does not, however, come straight from our genetic or biological background, nor is it a direct result of our environment. Each person is motivated to act because he can think, feel and process his world in a unique and personal way. Motivation emerges from a special combination of physical attributes, environment and individual emotional and perceptual qualities. Because we can perceive and represent situations symbolically, we can foresee the consequences of our own actions and those of other people, and thus alter our behavior, thoughts and emotions accordingly. In this way, people are motivated by their personal beliefs and values formed in their own mind. Yet, many of us come to similar beliefs and are motivated to work for similar goals such as world peace, elimination of sexism and racism, child advocacy and other important social causes.

Our motivations make up the reasons or "whys" of what we do. When we examine our motivation, we ask ourselves why? Why do we think, feel and talk as we do? What stimulates our thinking, feeling and talking? What pushes us and urges us to respond in the ways we do? What impels us to think, feel, act and talk? Whatare the purpose and intent of all our thoughts and actions?

Our motivation to think, feel and talk comes from the values and ideals we have developed over our lifetime. Motivation was a problem in Tina's family; her parents were motivated by inappropriate beliefs and ideals from their own childhood.

Tina was a frightened and unhappy child who needed a gentle touch and an open ear. Her parents were not motivated to provide this for her because they believed children should be tough, and should not be coddled or indulged.

Tina's parents confused positive and honest conversation with indulgence and spoiling. They did not value communication; they thought it was foolish and nonsensical. Positive communication was regarded as gibberish and people who did it were misinterpreted, mistrusted, and mocked. Tina's parents failed to communicate with her and pushed her out on her own because they were motivated by a philosophy that was insensitive and punitive. Tina's father believed that power, force and coercion were instrumental and effective means to get family members to obey him. Tina's mother was motivated to placate her volatile husband.

One of the many forces that serve to motivate people is a

belief in the human spirit. No matter what religion or source of spirituality you have accepted, striving to understand the human spirit can be seen as part of Abraham Maslow's idea of self-actualization, and this striving motivates us. Whether you are Roman Catholic, Muslim, Jewish, Eastern Orthodox, Protestant, Hindu, Buddhist, Baha'i or any other religion, the principles espoused will shape your motivation. The spiritual principles that most people share include honesty, justice, faithfulness, trustworthiness, kindness, caring and moderation.

If you are not a member of an organized religion, then your motivation and values will be shaped by your own sense of spirituality, your family, your culture, your education and other personal beliefs. All of these beliefs motivate and affect thinking, feeling and talking. People generally search for what is spiritual, truthful, benevolent, humanitarian and noble about human beings. Searching for goodness and wanting to do the right thing is healthy. The point is that we all search for meaning in life and move toward self-actualization. This search results in motivation, which shapes our thinking, feeling and talking. If our motivation is positive and genuine, the thinking, feeling and talking will work well for us. Motivation is the force that sets the thinking-feeling-talking wave in motion.

The second step in the communication model is thinking. After our motivations have been identified and put in order, we are inevitably going to be faced with a myriad of thoughts about the world. (Of course, our new thoughts about the world will go back and shape our motivation.) The human mind has to focus on some object, person or event before it can understand it or process it.

Motivation is like hunger; the image of an apple is the thought. Our thoughts and ideas come, in part, from our motivations.

Tina's experience can provide us with some examples of motivation and thinking. Tina is motivated to seek help in overcoming the bad feelings that have come from her childhood. She wants an adult to talk to her because she senses that through contact and caring can come resolution. Tina is able to stay with her "talk to me" need and not give up hope that talking is helpful, perhaps even lifesaving.

Thus, motivation to talk, seek answers, and stay in touch with her real feelings leads Tina to want conversation. Before Tina feels bad about her difficult situation she has done some thinking.

She thinks, "I am a bad person because I am stupid, mean and vain."

So the more she thinks she is bad, the worse she feels about it. That is why the adult she is speaking to is trying to get her to change her thinking. Tina is motivated to work on her problems so she continues to talk with the adult. As a young girl, she is able to understand that the adult is good even though she makes mistakes, but she has a harder time thinking that she is good in spite of her mistakes because she has been abused.

Consider this more simple example of thinking that precedes feeling. John has to see the large Mack truck speeding toward him and his daughter before he realizes they are in danger and he had better do something about it fast. John has no problem with the motivation to keep himself and his daughter safe. Thus, following motivation, in our communication model, comes perception or realization, which is, basically, thinking. We have to have a thought in our mind before we can understand it, react to it or talk about it.

Once John thinks about the truck zooming toward him and his daughter he feels fear. This is the third step in the process. He has an emotional reaction to the thought, "There is a large truck speeding toward me and my daughter." This feeling motivates him to grab his daughter's arm and run. As he swiftly moves to safety, he may yell to his daughter, "Move! There's a truck in the road!" John's words to his daughter complete the process of thinking-feeling-talking and, of course, the cycle starts again with new thoughts, feelings and words.

Let's try another example. Susan is motivated by friendship and the playground. She sees her friends playing jump rope on the playground at school. Her thinking about the scene of girls playing jump rope goes like this, "I did not know they were going to play jump rope today." This thought is step two in the motivation-thinking-feeling-talking process.

Her motivation to have friends would be step one. Step two involves a thought about what is happening to a person or what she sees. And next, step three, comes her feeling, "I am sad they did not tell me about the jump rope game, but I know they will let me join in now that I am here." Susan approaches her friends and asks if she can join the game and this begins step four, which is talking. She explains that she is late because she did not know they were going to get a game going today. Step four is the end point of the cycle as Susan explains her situation to her friends.

You are probably thinking that motivation-thinking-feeling-talking cannot possibly be so simple, neat and clean. You are right. This process is not simple or clear-cut because motivations, thinking, feeling and talking all occur continually, and different cycles overlap others. This all happens very rapidly within a person's mind, with motivations, thoughts, feelings and words all circling around and influencing each other continually. A psychologist would say that the motivation-thinking-feeling-talking process is both continual and recursive. Feelings emerge from our thoughts more quickly than we can keep track of at times and these feelings lead to more thoughts. When we decide to speak, it is hard to know exactly which thoughts and feelings prompted the statement. And, with each statement and chance to listen more thoughts and feelings come rolling through our mind. The human brain is a busy place, and the motivation-thinking-feeling-talking cycle spins endlessly around. It is no wonder we can sometimes l ose track of our thoughts and feelings.

A diagram may help to explain the motivation-thinking-feeling-talking cycle better. First comes motivation, which fuels our conscious effort to act. Motivation is in column one. In column two we can see that thoughts come next. From our thoughts we develop feelings or emotional reactions to what we perceive.

Column two illustrates an important part of the communication model, which is that feelings do not come out of nowhere; feelings come from the way we view the world. Our emotions come from our thoughtful observations of life around us. For example, if we believe that children are basically good human beings who need some guidance and training, then we will treat them with kindness and understanding as we discipline them within clear and firm limits. Before psychologists began to understand the motivation-thought-feeling relationship, some people believed that feelings came from the viscera and were separate from the brain. We now understand that our motivations and thoughts come first. Our feelings come about from our thoughts, and what we say is determined by our motivations, thoughts and feelings. Tina's mother believed that children were born with bad traits that would show up in their behavior unless they were severely punished. When she saw Tina brushing her hair she would say, "You are so vain and you have nothing to be vain about." Her motivation to speak this way came from her negative view of human nature, spurred by her thought, "Tina is brushing her hair again and that means she will be vain. I better teach her a lesson." This would lead to the criticism about vanity that hurt Tina so deeply.

To drive home the idea that feelings do not spontaneously generate inside of a person, let me give another example. Keep in mind that feelings come about from the motivations we gather during our life and from the thinking patterns we develop. Penny, a young mother, told me that she was sad. She did not know why she was sad; she felt as though she was born a sad and lonely person. She felt that unhappy feelings just swelled up inside of her and there was nothing she could do about it. After the birth of her two children, her sadness intensified. Still, she thought it was her lot in life to suffer from this sadness that she tried to keep a secret from most people. Sadness, she surmised, came from nowhere and she felt shame for having these feelings. She worried because her sadness rendered her unable to talk to her children some of the time.

When I spoke with Penny I listened to her carefully and asked her to explain her motivations, thoughts and feelings to me. I felt for her sadness and pain and told her that I would like to make some suggestions that might help her. I asked her if we could examine the idea of "feelings-from-nowhere" and she agreed. We looked into her past and found that her parents did everything for her and loved her in such an anxious, over-protective and critical way that she concluded she could not do anything right including raise her two children. I asked Penny to do an assignment at home during the next week before I saw her again. Her job was to identify in her daily thoughts all those that undermined her ability to cope. She made long lists of negative thoughts and then together we examined them to make them more accurate and moderate. As she changed some of the thoughts that undercut her ability to function and make decisions, she began to feel better. As she felt better, she began to deal with her children more confidently and consciously. So much for the feelings-from-nowhere idea.

Here are some of the negative thoughts that caused Penny to feel so bad:

Negative Thoughts

1. I better not try to find that new store I want to go to because I will probably get lost.

2. I cannot call my neighbor down the street to come to visit me because she probably won't like me anyway.

3. I'm going to give up on using time-out with my son; it doesn't work anyway.

4. I'm not going to bother to read my children a book today, they just wiggle and squirm and drive me crazy.

Penny needed some help to rework these negative thoughts because they prevented her from taking action that would help her to feel better and meet some of her goals in life. For instance, Penny was motivated to be more independent and try to go places without her husband driving her there. But statements like number 1 above undermined her confidence to try to drive to a new place. Penny reconstructed her thoughts in this way:

New Thoughts

1. If I get a map and check out the route with my husband tonight maybe I will try to find that new store tomorrow. If I get lost, I can ask at a gas station for directions.

2. Some people will like me and some people will not like me, that is how it goes with everyone. If I try to befriend my neighbor, the worst that could happen is that she could refuse. Then I will know to go seek out a different person. I do not have to conclude that I am unworthy, just that we did not match.

3. I want to help my son with his behavior problems. My doctor said to use time-out, but maybe I am not using it correctly. I better get a book or discuss it with someone who knows.

4. All children wiggle and squirm, and some don't even seem to care about books, but I read that a parent should read to them anyway. Some information gets in there even if the child does not look attentive. Also, children come to expect that I will sit with them and cuddle them during reading time. They are bound to get something good out of reading time.

After Penny changed some of her thinking patterns she began to feel better and try to do more of the activities that she enjoyed. There was also a change in the way she began to communicate. Before she spoke she considered her motivation, reworked her thinking, checked to see if her feelings were real (not just pretend) and then she spoke. These are some examples of how her talking improved:

Positive Communication

1. (To her husband) "I think I will go to that new fabric store in Hanover. Would you look at this map with me and see if you think I have picked out a good route?"

2. (To her neighbor) "Hello, this is Penny, your neighbor down the street, I wonder if you would like to come over tomorrow morning for a cup of tea. I would like to get to know you and I thought our children could play together."

3. (To her son) "I am going to put you in this corner when I hear bad talking. This is called time-out and this is a timer. You

cannot talk or move in time-out, or I will give you more time in the corner. The timer will keep track for us."

4. (To both children) "I am going to read this interesting book that I got from the library for you. While I read you can sit here with me or play quietly. Look at this great big monkey! What do you think he will do in this story?"

(Penny ignores the child doing somersaults in front of her, and he eventually wanders over to look at the picture.)

In column three of the model, you can see that we put our thoughts into words inside our head and this is referred to as self-talk. Pretty much everybody talks to himself inside without uttering a single word with his mouth. As a matter of fact, adults and children both talk to themselves frequently each day. In column three, you can also see that feelings, once they come from thoughts, are put into words in our heads as well. So naturally we talk to ourselves about our feelings. This is all private, and before they are allowed out of our mouths we may choose to filter and edit them. Some of our thoughts and feelings pass inspection and are sent out through our mouth or pen to be shared with other people. Some do not make it out. This model explains how communication works, and it is also a way to understand how thinking-feeling and talking can go wrong.

For Tina as a young child, thoughts and feelings got all mixed up and there was no adult around to help her straighten them all out. Most children who are abused come to the erroneous conclusion that there is something terribly wrong with them. They are too young to realize that bad things happen to children, but that does not mean they are bad. This self-doubt and self-hate is both the epitome and the irony of child abuse. Children are unable to understand the reasons for the abuse; they cannot see that their parent's abusive behavior is about the parent's own frustration and personal failure. In the motivation-thinking-feeling-talking cycle, you can see that Tina's childhood thought, "I am a bad person", led to feeling very bad about herself. She was convinced she was stupid, mean and vain (step two-thinking) which left her feeling worthless (step three-feeling). The next logical step for Tina was to withdraw; she was unable to communicate with people (step four-talking). If our make-believe adult were to question Tina about this, it would have gone something like this:

Adult: You know we can both agree now that you are a good person. I wonder if that changes any of your feelings about yourself? If you know you are good, then when your parents are mean to you or fighting with each other, I wonder if you can tell yourself that their problems do not mean that you are a bad person. Their problems only mean that they have confusion and trouble inside themselves.

Tina: You mean I do not cause my parents' problems? You mean they would have those problems and yell and hit even if I was perfect?

Adult: Yes, Tina, they have their own problems that are separate from you, even if those problems do hurt you. You are a good person whether you are abused by them or not. Can you keep that in your mind? Can you remember at all times that their problems do not change you into a bad person?

Tina: I can try. Then I won't be so scared all the time.

Adult: Can you keep these thoughts in your mind and make a soft and comfortable place inside of yourself? These thoughts will always be there inside you to use anytime you need them.

Tina: You mean make a safe and snuggly place inside myself where I can hear your voice and remember that these ideas are true?

Adult: Yes. You can make a safe and tender spot inside, and that is the beginning of growing what adults call a "secure inner life." When you think of yourself as a good person and find your warm spot inside, then you will not feel so sad all the time. Maybe if you do not feel so sad all the time, like at school, you might act differently in school? What would you do in school if you felt happy?

Tina: I would play jump rope with the girls and I would paint.

Adult: Since you know you are a good person now, maybe you will feel happier at school. Maybe you can think about being a good person and make some good feelings inside yourself. Maybe you could talk to a girl just like you. You might want to ask her to jump rope with you. Is that possible?

Tina: Do you think I could do that? Do you think JoAnn would want to jump rope with me?

Adult: Yes, I do think she would.

Tina: Maybe I will try to talk to her.

Notice here that as Tina starts to think of herself as a good person, she can start to solve her other problems. And, equally important, she can start to feel better about herself. This is the motivation-thinking-feeling part of the process, the first three steps. If this goes well it is almost inevitable that Tina will start talking to other people (step four) and begin to get involved in school. As we know this did not happen for Tina and because she did not get the communication that she needed she was not able to open up and relax during her elementary school years.

The motivation-thinking-feeling-talking cycle takes place within each person as they grow from infancy to adulthood. When a baby is born, he uses his senses to look at, touch, hear and taste the world around him. These early sensory experiences lay the foundation for his later thinking. As mentioned earlier, thinking is made up of sensations and perceptions, so all the rich and varied experiences of the newborn baby come together to determine what is going on in his mind. As with adults, a baby must be aware of some sensation or perception before he has a feeling. The sensation of hunger makes the baby feel upset, then he begins to cry.

One line of evidence that lets psychologists know they are on the right track is that babies first develop thinking about whether objects exist before they ever utter their first word. That is, infants have to know that things and people are separate from themselves and permanent out there in the world before they can begin to label objects and people. To a baby, a ball is not a ball until he knows it continues to exist even though it rolled behind a chair. When the baby knows enough to go search for the ball, he will be able to learn the word "ball." So, clearly, in infant development, thinking comes first. Then, talk emerges, based on the thinking that has led the way. And, in line with those ideas, the thinking about the ball comes first, the desire to have the ball comes next, and the word to label the ball comes last.

In the chapters that follow this motivation-thinking-feeling-talking process will be described more fully and it will be used to explain how to improve parent-child communication. This has been an introduction to the motivation-thinking-feeling-talking process. But at this point, with some basic understanding of the routine of motivation-thinking-feeling-talking, it may be time to ask why bother with all of this. Let's pause and ask why deal with this complicated communication model.

What are the advantages for us in understanding more about how our motivation, thoughts, feelings and talk all work together to make communication?

Why am I putting this effort into exploring motivation-thinking-feeling-talking and asking you to come along?

There are two reasons. The first reason: healthy communication can potentially hold the human family together. Effective communication and language can bond people together whether we are talking about the human race or our own individual families. Second, effective communication can cut through barriers like an ax through a log. There are young children who spend many days, weeks or even months inside their homes frightened of dogs or bugs or men with hats. As with Tina, there are many children who feel isolated and alone without help with their troubles. There is no better way to short-circuit their fear and isolation than to get them to talk and work on the problem with an adult.

Language as a Bond

People have been talking to each other, or trying anyhow, for thousands and thousands of years. This probably has something to do with the cultural, scientific and technological progress we have made during the millennia. There is no doubt that language is a powerful, interactive force that allows human connections that would, without it, remain primitive. Imagine having a relationship with your mother, son or neighbor that did not include language? Some people might think that living without language would be easier, simpler, and more peaceful. But what do we do automatically when something frightening happens to us? We go immediately and directly to our closest friend and tell him all about our fear, expecting to be listened to and given words of comfort and sympathy. This would be impossible without language.

Language has a civilizing effect on human beings. Language has developed and become more sophisticated along with our advancing world. Long ago, different writers spelled words according to their whim; they defined words with less precision than we currently require. But now every school child knows there is a correct spelling and definition for each word; we use a more sophisticated language system than people used even a century ago.

Language allows people to come face to face with each other and exchange meaning and feeling. There are few times when we come face to face with people, have direct eye contact, and remain physically close to them without saying something to them. It feels good to be close to people, and talking to them is a central part of being close. Only people who are about to have a fistfight or who are infatuated with each other spend time staring into each other's eyes without talking.

Conversation is fun, even if it can be sticky like glue, bonding people together. Talking with friends, family and just about anybody else can be more entertaining than a lot of other activities that take lots of effort and money. Mortimer J. Adler, a writer and philosopher, wrote:

"The leisure pursuits that are preeminently social include all acts of friendship and, above all, conversation in its many forms. In my judgment, engaging in good conversation - talk that is enjoyable and rewarding - is one of the very best uses that human beings can make of their free time."

Language breaks down barriers

Have you ever been seated close to someone who speaks another language? It's hard to get beyond the smile and nod stage. There is usually a desire to communicate in some way from both parties, but short of grunting or making primitive gestures, there is a barrier. We wonder what the other person is thinking about us. A quick sideways glance from our nonverbal companion may prompt the thought, "Maybe she doesn't like my shirt, my hair, my smile or ...me?"

Our vulnerable thought may lead to some uncomfortable feelings of self-doubt, or we might just feel boredom, frustration or perhaps even relief for having a few quiet moments. But without a doubt it is impossible to express what we are thinking or feeling to the other person and it is equally difficult to know what he or she is experiencing.

Compare this uncommunicative situation with one where you begin to talk to a stranger. An amazing amount of information comes out quickly, some intentional and some not. We can sense whether they want to talk to us, whether they are friendly or reserved, loquacious or reticent, polished or earthy. And, of course, we can be wrong about the conclusions we come to on the basis of the first conversation. Nonetheless, at least when there is conversation, there is data to work on and we can develop our communication from there.

To conclude this chapter, let me summarize the motivation-thinking-feeling-talking process and why it is important. The key that turns on the ignition (thinking) is motivation; it is the urge and the impetus. Thinking is the second step in communication between people. It is the substance of our talk, and it guides the direction of our talk. It is by no means the most important aspect of talk; it is just the beginning. Feelings play an equally important role in people's speech, and they are often strong motivators in encouraging people to talk. Feelings can be so strong that they move us to talk even if we are naturally shy or quiet. Feelings can also be so overwhelming that they seem to come out of the blue. Children and adults have told me that they have no idea where their feelings came from. More feelings-from-nowhere. They swear that their feelings have a life of their own and are uncontrollable.

It takes some detective work, but feelings can be traced back to thoughts. Thoughts can be modified and changed, based on new information and insight. When the thoughts are changed, modified, or toned down to match reality the feelings follow along. When we are calm and rational, we know that moderation in our view of people and events will serve us well. We know that to think about situations in life in extreme or catastrophic ways only makes our feelings reel out of control along with our thoughts. Then it is difficult or even impossible to talk in a reasonable or moderate way. So, the task for both children and adults in their development is to perceive events in the most accurate and moderate way possible. This takes some work and usually does not happen automatically. But it is worth the effort.

"Whosoever passeth beyond the limits of moderation will cease to exert a beneficial influence...If carried to excess, civilization will prove as prolific a source of evil as it had been of goodness when kept within the restraints of moderation...All other things are subject to this principle of moderation." (Baha'u'llah Gleanings 216,342)

Adler, Mortimer J. *How to Speak, How to Listen.* Macmillian, New York, 1983, p. 17.

Beck, Aaron T. *Love is Never Enough.* Harper and Row Publishers, New York, 1988, p.2.

Burns, David *The Feeling Good Handbook* Penguine Books, New York, 1990.

Bah'u'llah *Gleanings From The Writings of Baha'u'llah.*

Maslow, Abraham *Motivation and Personality.* Harper and Row, New York, 1970 (2nd edition).

Meichenbaum, D. *Cognitive-behavior Modification: An integrative approach.* Plenum Press, New York, 1977.

Weiner, Bernard *Theories of Motivation.* Rand McNally, Chicago, 1972.

Chapter 2

Keep Talking, Mom and Dad!

"Children have to work out the way in which language is organized for themselves and, fortunately, they are well equipped to do so. But they can't do it all on their own."
-Gordon Wells

Even newborn babies want to get in on conversation. When you get within a foot of a newborn baby's face and speak to him in a slow, clear manner with a high pitched voice, he is likely to give you his full attention and gaze right into your eyes. He will look at you and give you his full attention if he is not tired, hungry, or frustrated. He will even sustain interest in your face and voice for quite a few seconds, if not minutes. This is the beginning of many groundbreaking conversations.

So newborns are ready to go eyeball to eyeball. This is groundbreaking because once you have the baby's attention you can provide for him the much-needed food for thought that comes from conversation. The baby is being treated by you to wonderful sounds for his ears and a feast for his eyes. Babies need rich and varied sensory stimulation to get their brains in gear. A great deal of research has demonstrated that babies who are presented with interesting sounds, faces, objects, colors, shapes, and movements learn more and mature earlier. So thinking can begin as early as birth, given the necessary face to face lessons.

Another exciting aspect of the newborn-adult conversation is the rhythmic, ping pong-like quality of the interaction. Babies are getting the hang of back and forth conversation. Infants that are spoken to early in their life begin to talk back to their parents. Of course this is not the kind of back-talk that will occur when they are thirteen years old, rather it is the basis of all conversation where each speaker takes his turn and then waits for his partner to respond.

Newborns are so small and fragile that they do not seem to be aware of their surroundings. Will they remember all the touching, thinking, feeling, and talking that is going on around them? Will all of this make a difference in their lives? Why don't we just aim to keep them safe and breathing and wait until they grow up?

The answers to these questions are a matter of life and health. The quality of the care an infant receives stays with him throughout his life. Each developmental step he takes and the responsivity of the people around him will contribute to how he perceives and values himself and other people. An infant's ability to perceive the world brings up the question of whether or not he can remember it. There is ample evidence in the psychological literature to show that infants remember what happens to them. They also remember how they feel about what happens. One teenage girl looked at an old bedspread at a friend's house and remarked to her mother, "I recognize that floral pattern. Didn't we use to have a bedspread like that?" Her mother was shocked and replied, "Yes, we did but you were only an infant when I had that bedspread on my bed. I think I got rid of it when you were about a year old."

Not only do we remember the sights, sounds, and smells around us when we are babies, but we remember the most important aspects of our lives: how we are treated by the people around us. If infants are treated with love, they come to know what love feels. If infants are treated with kindness and caring, they came to know how kindness feels. And if babies are treasured and valued, they grow to feel important and valuable.

"Who are you talking to?" asked David, our carpenter and friend, as he walked into the kitchen for a drink. David was working on the outside of our house and came into the house occasionally over the course of the morning. He heard me talking and assumed there was another adult or child somewhere in the house. He knew I had a baby and that she was just a few weeks old. David was not yet a father, so had not had the opportunity to be instructed by a small person weighing only eight pounds and using mostly gurgles and grunts for language. That is when he decided to ask me to whom I was talking. Of course my baby girl was perched in an infant seat in front of me, inviting me to speak to her by looking at me with an incredibly cute smile. So I finally answered his question in a most matter of fact way.

"My baby, of course."

I said this as though he should have known. David just shook his head and went back out to nail up some shingles.

Everyone has probably seen parents talking to their newborn, waiting for him to gurgle, and then responding as if he had said something profound. A lot of feeling and information is exchanged even though the infant does not use words. In the last two decades, researchers have studied infants' conversational ability. This research highlights the exquisite communication process that develops between typically eager parents and their responsive infants. Mothers and fathers communicate with their infants in ways that encourage them to use the senses they are born with. These senses are vital to infant thinking because they are like the mail carriers of information from the outside world to infant's mind. When we understand the infant's senses and how they are used, then we can more easily view them as the building blocks of thought.

Let's start with sight. Newborn babies can see clearly for about ten to twelve inches, which is the distance between him and his mother's face during feeding. Adults also tend to move their faces about twelve inches from the newborn's face when they say hello and start a conversation. By six weeks of life, the thick lens of the newborn eye begins to thin out and he can focus his eyes at a greater distance. Imagine how exciting the world looks to him as he can focus on objects and events further from him. Perhaps it is not an accident that the infant is exposed to gradually more and more complex sights as he gets older. Too much too fast could be overly stimulating.

What does this tell us about infant thinking and seeing? If you want the newborn to see you or something you want to show him, consider his age and the right distance for his eyes. You may want to hang a mobile in his crib or show him Aunt Edna's face but before six weeks you will have to come within a foot of the baby's eyes. Once a baby is able to see further away you will find him gazing out beyond your arms and the crib. Put some wonderfully bright and interesting shapes around, especially faces and the color red.

Five months before birth, infants' hearing is fully functioning. The ossicles or small bones of the inner ear are the only bones completely formed before birth. This means that the fetus can hear inside the uterus for four months before birth. Newborns hear quite well. I spoke with a young mother who had her second baby when I was in the hospital having my first. I spoke softly to her so as not to disturb the baby, which was asleep in her arms.

"Oh, don't worry, babies can't hear for a long time after they are born," she said. I responded gently not knowing how she would feel about the news I had to share.

"Actually babies can hear quite well at birth, except for a bit of water in their ears. As a matter of fact, your baby already likes your voice because she has been listening to it for four months already."

"Is this your first baby?" she countered skeptically.

Research on infant hearing has demonstrated that at six weeks infants are able to distinguish between a "p" and "b" sound. An infant is given a pacifier to suck as he hears a tape recording of the "pa" sound. He stops sucking for a few seconds to listen to the sound. Then as the sound is repeated, he resumes sucking. The "ba" sound is presented and the infant stops sucking again. In this way, we can tell that infants notice changes in sound. Infants cannot tell us what they know about sounds and voices, but we can infer from their behavior that they notice subtle differences.

Babies like to hear people talk far better than listening to plain sounds. Not only do infants like the sound of the human voice but they actually show a preference for their mother's when they are three days old. Babies are born with a sensitivity to language right from birth.

The senses of touch, smell, and taste are working well at birth and babies use them all to communicate. The newborn can hear voices, see faces, make eye contact, feel skin contact, smell his mother, and taste her milk. Although babies are able to use their senses when parents talk to them, they may not always be in the mood for a conversation. Just like their mothers may, babies change moods. Infants typically cycle through five moods or states a day.

1. Deep regular sleep occurs when the infant breathes regularly and does not move except for startles. The infant's eyes are closed.

2. Active irregular sleep includes irregular breathing and small movements. The infant's eyes sometimes open briefly.

3. Alert inactivity is when the infant is wide-awake, with eyes open but making no large movements.

4. Alert activity is a state where the infant is awake and moving.

5. Crying includes loud, distress calls with vigorous movements.

Perhaps these moods that babies cycle through have some relationship to the moods and feelings they will have later in life. As an adult, imagine how it feels when your spouse looks at you as you walk in the door from an exceptionally long day at work, and he says to you, "Gee, you look tired and hungry. I saved some dinner for you and I got the kids sitting in the dining room doing their homework." This kind of a greeting feels so good. When our moods or feelings are acknowledged and responded to, we can stay in touch with our feelings and value them as they guide us through our contact with people and the world. The tired wife can accept that she is tired, take a few minutes to eat and unwind, and then talk with her family to see how they feel and how their day went. When we accept our feelings and moods, we learn that our feelings are an asset to help us make sense out of our own behavior and what is happening around us.

In infancy, the same kind of trust in feelings begins to grow. The baby cries. This signals the father. He feels concern for the baby and he goes to pick him up. From this comfort the baby learns that his feelings matter. From birth all the way on through the adolescent years, the way parents respond to their children's feelings and moods will determine the extent to which they can tune into and understand their own feelings. If a baby gives a sharp cry of pain, the mother looks quickly for an open pin or some other source of injury. If a toddler protests the touch of a stranger, the parents respond swiftly to comfort the child. If a child shows anxiety about school, the parents respond by checking out the situation. If a teenager acts sad, the parents respond to those feelings and offer help. To the extent that parents respond to their children's feelings and moods with thinking and feeling responses, the children stay connected with their feelings and trust their feelings. This is the foundation for self-confidence.

Abused children grow to be adults who are incapable of knowing what they feel. It has been documented that adults who were emotionally, physically, and sexually abused cannot accurately label and identify their feelings. One of the main goals of psychotherapy with adults abused as children is to help them to understand what they feel. Consider the motivation-thinking-feeling-talking model. If an adult does not know what he feels, then the cycle is always short-circuiting around feeling step three.

When Tina was a child she did not understand why she did not like her father to "tickle" her. Her father took each of her sisters in turn, threw them on the floor and then tickled them very hard. He put his hands under their shirts and pants and tickled them until they could not talk or breathe. He thought this was great fun. Tina felt shortness of breath, rapid heart beat and like her stomach had turned to lead when she saw this was starting to happen. Her father would pull her down on the carpet and tell her it was her turn. She could not protest or she would be punished; her father told her that this was fun, and this is how he paid attention to her.

Communication cannot go well if a person does not know what he feels. We are examining how babies learn to connect with their feelings. They use their senses, they are allowed to experience moods, they learn to trust their feelings and they learn that a loving adult will respond to their needs and feelings.

When parents accept children's feelings they listen and acknowledge, but this is not to be confused with indulgence and permissiveness. We listen to why a boy is angry with his brother, but we do not allow him to call names or hit. We tell the boy that we want to know what he thinks and how he feels but he must express those feelings without harming other people. We tell our daughter that it is good when we are visiting friends to tell us that she is bored and wants to go home, but she cannot whine or say rude things.

After a long nap, a warm bath and a good meal, babies are ready for talk. They are usually in the alert inactive or alert active state. They like people to come close and talk with a high pitched voice. Mothers typically keep their turn short so that the baby has a chance to respond. Babies know just what to do when it's time to talk: they make eye contact, they move their limbs, and they coo and smile. By six weeks old, they are pretty accomplished talkers. Mothers tend to synchronize their talking with the baby's sounds and movement.

Cooing and smiling are heart-warming but good moods do not last forever. Once a baby cries, parents who respond quickly and consistently have infants who cry less. Note that this is true for every age starting in infancy and continuing through the teens: parents who talk to their children about what is bothering them are likely to have emotionally well-functioning children. Thus, crying is a signal the baby uses to let his parents know he needs help. Emotional upset or complaints are signals children use to signal distress. A baby cannot say, "I'm ready for lunch now" but he can let out a wail that alerts Mom to figure out what he wants. A preschool age child cannot say, "I am angry because you have not spent quality time with me today" but he can pout and cry. Likewise, adolescents have a hard time saying, "I feel misunderstood, so can you sit and show me some empathy and understanding?" but instead may act out pain or hurt.

I am surprised by the number of children and adolescents I have seen who were clinically depressed and without their parents being aware of it. The responsivity of the parents in infancy has some relationship to how responsive the parents will be as their children grow older. There will be difficulties and challenges in every child's life and that is something parents cannot prevent. What parents can do is stay alert to the emotional responses of their children and discuss them as they arise. Psychologists know that mental illness in childhood comes about when pain and problems go unacknowledged and unaccepted. Children can endure great hardship and trauma when there is a loving and responsive adult to buffer the pain and usher in the healing.

By four to five weeks of age infants begin to make sweet cooing sounds, like the long "u" sound. Cooing is usually a pleasant, lyrical sound, but can involve gurgles also. In any case, cooing gives way to babbling by four to five months of age. Babbling is a language-like series of sounds that can be either monotone or have an intonational rise and fall. There are some sounds that are not produced by babbling babies including "str" as in stripe and "ngth" as in strength. Yet, there is a remarkable array of sounds produced, and these sounds are not limited to the language the baby hears around him. There are two sounds that are produced frequently by babbling babies, but as children begin to speak they are slow to make these sounds: "l" and "r."

I found that if I put a teddy bear, with a face that is big and

28

clear, two round, dark eyes, a red nose and a smiley mouth, my babies would spend some time after they woke up babbling to their teddy bear. Sometimes, they would babble to the mobile of clown faces that hung over their crib. It helps a baby to grow mentally to have many bright and interesting objects to look at. It may also encourage babies to babble more when they are given stimulating things to look at. When they babble they often focus on an object and appear to be talking to it. It is endless fun to spy on them when they are alone babbling; they can look so serious and engrossed in what sounds like a conversation.

As the baby approaches nine months, the sounds he produces will begin to sound more like his native language. He hears his parents and other people talking and his babbling comes to incorporate the sounds he hears. The baby begins to eliminate some babbling sounds that he produced earlier but does not hear in the language around him. After the baby has acquired his first words, he may continue to babble for some time. Often babies babble when they are alone as in the morning when they wake up. Babies babble in similar ways. There is a preponderance of middle vowel sounds, soft consonants like "b" and "m", and hard consonants like "g".

As a baby begins to crawl during his eighth month, he becomes actively involved in everything around him. Among other things, animals, toys, knickknacks, clothing, and kitchen appliances are all fair game for touching. Babies learn by crawling around, exploring movement, and touching objects. Hand in hand with babies' newfound locomotion comes an explosion of thinking: the baby is about to remember that if his bottle drops on the floor, it is not gone forever. This is called object permanence. Object permanence is the gradual realization that objects exist even when they are out of sight. It is the most important intellectual achievement of the first year of life, and it is vital to the acquisition of language. Without object permanence, a child cannot speak his first word.

At the time my son, Kirk, acquired object permanence, we were given a wooden toy with four holes in which to put four balls. The balls were too big to swallow and they were colorful. Kirk loved this toy and when it was first presented to him he literally shook with delight. As his little hand placed each ball in a hole, he would tremble with glee as it rolled down an incline and came out at the bottom. My problem was that the balls would roll out of the toy and under the furniture. Because Kirk had object permanence, he would crawl to the spot where the ball was last seen and wail. I had to move the couch, chairs, oven drawer and even the refrigerator once, to find these precious balls.

Object permanence grows slowly in the child's awareness from the moment of birth when he sees his mother's face and hears her voice. It is the awareness that objects and people exist independently of the infant's existence. Imagine dangling a squeaky, red, toy mouse in front of a six-month-old. Most likely, he will grasp it. Remove the mouse from his grasp and hide it behind a blanket. He will not scream or cry or even search for it. But at eight months old, the baby will act puzzled and search when the toy is removed. This is the dawning of object permanence because the baby remembers the toy and thinks about where it is. Person permanence develops along with object permanence. A five-month-old baby will not cry when his mother leaves, but a nine-month old will protest loudly.

Language Building Ideas
Before birth:

1. Babies in utero can hear at age five months, so, parents, start talking to your baby while he is inside the womb. He will listen to your words and learn from all the sounds you expose him to including music, conversation, waterfalls, and animal sounds. He will grow accustomed to your voice and will prefer to hear it over other voices. Speak slowly and clearly in short phrases with a high-pitched, rising intonation when you are talking to him.

2. Play music before the baby is born and repeat the same music as the months go by.

After birth:

3. Continue to talk to your baby. But now you have the added bonus of eye contact and touching. Look at your baby and rub, stroke and tickle him while you continue to talk in short high-pitched phrases.

4. Use the baby's name in songs, rhymes, and chants, so that he will begin to recognize it.

5. Continue to play music and sing to your baby.

Timing:

6. Note your baby's mood to see when he is ready for conversation. You can have long (5 to 10 minutes) interchanges when he is in the alert active and alert inactive states.

7. When he is crying or distressed sing to him and gently soothe him with your voice.

8. Anytime you talk to him be sensitive to his timing. Let him "talk" for as long as he wants to. Then respond to him. Let down your inhibitions and say all kinds of descriptive and adoring things to him. But when he begins to take his turn in conversation, stop and let him go. This is how he will learn the turn-taking rhythm of conversation.

Object Permanence:

9. Names object and say what they are many times. Make a game of it: This is a ball. Ball, ball, ball! Can you say ball? Repeat this little song with different objects throughout the day.

10. Hide objects under a cloth or behind a board and make them appear. Describe what you are doing in simple talk: Here is your doll! See her! Now watch, she is going under the blanket. Where is she? Oh! Here she is!

11. Animal noises are lots of fun. Associate the animal with the proper sound. Ask the baby, "Can you say kitty? The kitty says meow. Meow. Meow. Meow."

Person Permanence:

12. Give people names and repeat them for your baby, especially your names, Mommy and Daddy!

13. Sing your names and family member's names going up the musical scale and then back down. Babies love the rising pitch! And they love to hear their family's names as well as their own.

14. Play peek-a-boo and hide and seek. These old classics have been passed down for centuries for a reason; they help children develop person permanence.

Sharing Books

15. By the time your baby is six months old he will enjoy looking at books with you for brief periods of time. Sit close to him, enjoy the intimacy, and describe the pictures to him.

References

Bebee, Beatrice, Sterns, Daniel and Jaffe, Joseph *The Kinesic Rhythm of Mother-Infant Interactions.* In Seigman, Aron and Feldstein, Stanley (eds) Of Speech and Time, John Wiley and Sons, New York, 1979.

Crystal, David *Listen to your child.* Penguine Books, England, 1986.

DeCasper, A.J., and Fifer, W.P. *Of Human Bonding: Newborns prefer their mothers' voices.* Science, 1980, 208, 1174-1176.

Eimas, P.D. *Speech Perception in Early Infancy.* In L.B. Cohen and P. Salapetek (eds) I*nfant Perception: From Sensation to Cognition* (Vol 2) Academic Press, New York, 1975.

Ginsburg, G.P. and Kilbourne, B.K. *Emergence of vocal alternation in mother-infant interchanges.* Journal of Child Language, 15, 1988, 221-235.

Gopnik, A. and Meltzoff, A. *The development of categorization in the second year and its relation to other cognitive and linguistic developments.* Child Development, 1987, vol 58, 1523-1531.

Levitt, M.J., Antonucci, T.C. and Clark M.C. *Object-person permanence and attachment: another look.* Merrill-Palmer Quarterly, 1984, vol 30, 1-10.

Miller, Alice *For Your Own Good: Hidden Cruelty in Child-rearing.* Penguine Books, New York, 1985.

Tomasello, M. and Farrar, M. *Object permanence and relational words: A lexical training study.* Journal of Child Language, 1986, vol 13, 495-505.

Vander Zanden, James *Human Development*, Alfred A. Knopf, Inc., New York, 1981.

Wellman, H.M., Cross, D. and Bartsch, K. *Infant search and object permanence: A meta-analysis of the A-not-B error.* Monographs of the Society for Research in Child Development: 1987, vol 5, 1-51.

Wishart, J. and Bower, T.G. *A longitudinal study of the development of the object concept.* Special Issue: Infancy. British Journal of Developmental Psychology, 1985, vol 3, 243-258.

Wells, Gordon *The Meaning Makers: Children Learning Language and Using Language to Learn.* Heineman, Portsmouth, NH, 1986.

Wolff, P H (1966) *The causes, controls and organization of the behavior of the neonate.* Psychological Issues, 5, 1-105.

Chapter 3

The First Word

---

*"Thinking helps us to identify our feelings accurately,
to put them into perspective and to make healthy choices
about what to do with them. Talk them out? Act them
out? Let them be?"*

                                        -Linda T. Sanford

Parents of older children who have already passed the one-word stage may be tempted to skip this chapter. Please do not. I believe it would be useful to understand what you and your child have already been through, and I would like to explain why the efforts you have already put into teaching and talking with your youngster were important and successful. Parents benefit from knowing about the complex system they have already set in motion. Parents should understand and acknowledge their work so they can pat themselves on the back. Furthermore, there are some important points made in this chapter on the significance of words and how we use them with older children. We will touch on how using words can go wrong in some families.

When a one-year-old begins to speak, he tells what he knows of the world and how he feels about it. A child learns that his words can have an effect on people around him, and gains a sense of strength and control. A great deal of thinking and feeling come before the first word is spoken. By the time of a baby's first birthday, he will be using a recognizable word, and you can bet that he will use it again. Within a matter of days or weeks this child will have ten words at his command. In the next few months, his vocabulary will swell to about fifty words. Imagine what it must feel like to have fifty meaningful sounds at your disposal all of a sudden. Not only is the child able to say what he thinks, he can more accurately explain his feelings. In this chapter, we will look at the kind of freedom the child at the one-word stage has that he did not have before. A child at the one-word stage stands at the crossroads, where language can open up new worlds and emancipate him, or language can be used to hurt and denigrate him.

It is exhilarating when a baby begins to label things he sees. Naming objects becomes a pastime for baby, and he frequently uses the word for the object in a questioning tone for Mommy and Daddy to answer with an approving and confirming, "''Yes, Johnny, that's a kitty." Parents like to teach their child many new words in this way, but after the labeling of one hundred objects during breakfast alone this teaching process becomes less than exhilarating. When you are in the mood, the naming game helps thinking develop and it makes for some good feelings of accomplishment for both parent and child. About 50 percent of the words you will name with your baby are general terms and about 15 percent are specific names, such as Mommy, Fido, Jenny.

Action words are satisfying for a baby because he can do them as he says them. Needless to say, action words are tiring for Mom and Dad because they have to perform them too. But just think of the fun you will have as you pick up the teddy bear and say, "Up" or watch him fall and say, "Down." You may think your child will learn up and down after three trials. Not so. He will want to do this at least three dozen times. Other action words with appeal are: push, open, close, bye-bye. About 15 percent of the time, children spend working on action words.

Words that describe are important because they help convey

messages of both thoughts and feelings. Examples of describing words are: dirty, mine, Mommy, all gone, and more. Toddlers can be creative in their use of descriptors. My year old daughter stuffed a softball into a clear plastic container and exclaimed, "All gone" as though the ball was gone forever. She could not get the ball out so I had to get it out each of the three dozen times she tried it. We did this every day for several weeks and eventually all gone came to describe an object that was temporarily stuck. Children in the one word stage describe about 10 percent of the time. Function words that serve to get the job done include: no, please, what?, for, stop. Year-old children can accomplish a lot with one word, and they do this about 10 percent of the time.

When you consider the kinds of thinking and intention that go into talking with one word, it is amazing what the toddler can do. Practice with one word helps the child move toward combining two words. When we talk to our one-word children in short clear sentences, there is no doubt that they will eventually strive to put words together as we do.

During the one-word stage, words come to have a tremendous impact on the child's feelings as well as his intellectual and language development. If Mom tells a six-month-old infant he is stupid, he will recognize the scorn in Mom's face and in her voice but he will not understand what stupid means. At one year old, if Mom calls her child stupid, the child can grasp that stupid has a negative meaning and he will feel hurt. He will associate the word stupid with what he feels about himself and what he is capable of doing. "Stupid" becomes an automatic inner label and he will use it against himself; it will keep him from realizing his potential and developing self-confidence.

Toddlers are doers. First, they learn words that they can act on easily. Objects that the child can hold and manipulate catch his interest and he learns to label them. Shoes and socks are commonly among the child's first ten words because they can be pulled off and carried around. A child can help his mother take off his shoes and socks and he can put hers on her feet. There are many things to do with shoes and socks and all this action captures the child's imagination as well as occupies his busy hands. Hat is another fun object for taking on and off of Mom or Dad or anyone else. Hats can be placed on oneself or on other children or even on cats and dogs. It is the action involved that is fun, and this makes the word easier to learn. So any object that is small enough to be touched and moved is likely to be labeled early on.

Action and movement are vital to a child's development, and should be encouraged. Talk about action and movement taps into a child's natural motivation, thinking and feeling process. For instance, parents can comment, "I see you can run fast." "Look at how high you have climbed." "You have learned to climb up on the couch." "Let me see you throw the ball." "Good reaching and stretching." When parent comments in this fashion the child feels validated in his natural inclinations. When a child hears words such as the following he does not learn to trust his natural inclinations: "You never hold still—what is wrong with you?" "Stop moving so much." "You are too busy." "You are driving me crazy." "Why are you so hyper?" "Who wound you up?" A reasonable amount of movement and action is critical for development and provides great opportunities for talking. An active child must be distinguished from a misbehaving or hyperactive child. Don't hesitate to ask a heath care professional if you are not sure you understand and can recognize the difference.

Children do not hold still much. As we have seen, this abundant activity is helpful for learning words like shoes, socks, hats, balls, and kitty. The activity that toddlers and preschool age children engage in is fruitful because it helps them explore their world and learn about it. Each time a toddler touches a new object or sees something, it is a marvelous moment for Mom and Dad to teach using talk. Watching a car zoom past, little Johnny points and Mom says, "See the car go fast!" Johnny may say, "Car" and Mom reinforces with, "Yes, that's a car." The motivation-thinking-feeling-talking cycle is put into play during these parent-child conversations.

Mom's motivation to help Johnny learn language is part of her overall commitment to nurture him and educate him. So, she is motivated to teach him and to give him the message that his motivation, thinking, feeling and talking are important to her. As a matter of fact, Mom's early interactions with Johnny during the first six or seven years of his life will lay the foundation for both his intellectual and emotional development. The words she chooses to use with him will have a great impact on how he grows.

Words have potential to hurt. Once children understand that words have meaning they quickly acquire the meanings of many new words; their vocabulary grows exponentially. When negative words slip into a child's vocabulary, it is like letting him play with a loaded gun. Children can turn the words or gun upon themselves or upon other people. Negative words convey negative meaning about the child and diminish his feelings of self-worth. My oldest son Kirk was one year old the day he cried and fussed all during a four-hour car ride. I tried my best to comfort him within the constraints of a car seat. When we arrived at our destination, I was exhausted and emotionally drained, and he innocently started whining about a bottle of apple juice. I blurted out, "Shut up." as I prepared his bottle of apple juice and handed it to him. This happened twelve years ago but I remember it like it happened twelve minutes ago.

I thought about how I would feel if Kirk told himself to shut up, or if he told someone else to shut up. The moment he realized what shut up meant he would start to use it with possible hurtful consequences. I had a talk with Kirk at age one that he did not understand. I promised him (and me) that I would never say that to him again and instead would say, "Would you please be quiet?" Obviously I have used that sentence many times during the last twelve years, and each time, it has some special meaning for me.

Mom and Dad help Johnny to think and feel on a daily basis at the one word stage by labeling objects, feelings, and events. This expands his vocabulary. They are also teaching him to become interested in the physical and social world around him. Important feelings are exchanged between parent and child during talks about objects, feelings and events. As Mom and Dad show interest and pleasure in talking to Johnny, he realizes that they value him, his thoughts, his feelings and his words. He enjoys learning about the world and words, but he also likes their attention. This motivation-thinking-feeling-talking process becomes a challenging and satisfying means for learning and bonding.

The motivation-thinking-feeling-talking train becomes derailed when words hurt. The one word stage is an important juncture to examine words that hurt and how they wreak their havoc. Tina was told she was vain when she was young, and even though she was not sure exactly what that meant, she knew it was bad. Tina felt guilty. She chastised herself for having yet another bad quality and came to believe that vain was equivalent to worthless. This one hurtful word contributed greatly to Tina's low self-esteem and threatened her ability to trust herself. Words can damage children by the following sequence of events. The child thinks, "I am motivated to be a good child. I hear that my mother thinks that I am vain. I do not think I am vain, but my mother is sure about this; she is probably right. I better ignore my own belief and pay attention to her label. I feel terrible for being vain. I must be a bad person. There must be something wrong with me. I am not good enough to talk to people because I cannot trust what I think and feel. I cannot trust that I am not vain. I am ashamed. I do not dare to reveal my true thoughts."

A one-year-old child is a unique and special person already. The way each one-year old child will receive and process the hurtful words he hears will differ according to his temperament, personality, and life experience. Children, at any age, do not understand that mean words have more to do with the speaker than them. Children take mean talk personally and cannot imagine it comes from the speaker's personal problems. A word that hurts one child will not necessarily hurt another. Although we can all agree that words like stupid, shut-up, vain, idiot, jerk and retard are hurtful to children, there is a range of other words that can potentially lower children's self esteem. Words like slow, moody, crabby, get lost, know-it-all, bossy, selfish, and too sensitive are probably more subtly hurtful. They diminish a child's ability to feel confident. There is always a better, more specific way to say, "You are too slow this morning." Instead we can say, "I want you to brush your teeth in three minutes this morning." To replace, "Get lost—you are bugging me," we can say, "I need a few minutes alone. Please play downstairs for twenty minutes." As an alternative to, "You are too sensitive—just get out there and play with those kids," we can say, "I see that you are unsure of what to say, but I think whatever comes to your mind is fine to say to those kids."

Hurt feelings and emotional suffering are individual experiences. Words can trigger particular thoughts and feelings that may be painful to one person, but not to another. We need to teach our children to tell us if a word hurts or bothers them. We need to listen carefully to our children when a word is puzzling, painful, or confusing. We need to respect our children's individual rights to express how a word makes them feel. We need to look at their faces and bodies to see how our words affect them, and ask them to talk about it.

When we acknowledge our child's feelings about words, he becomes capable of trusting his own thoughts and feelings. He feels a sense of his own power in standing up for himself with words. A child must be able to say, "I don't like it when you call me slow," or, "Stop telling me I'm too emotional," or, "It hurts when you say I am vain." When a child is confident enough to respond to the words he hears, he will keep the lines of communication open with his parents. When a child cannot speak of what he feels and knows, he will shut down, withdraw, and distance himself from his parents. Start early in a child's life, start at the one word stage, to accept children's words. Pay close attention to the words you use with them. Do help the child to speak politely and with respect, but listen, accept and acknowledge the messages he sends.

41

The price parents pay for not listening, accepting and acknowledging is silence and resentment from their children. Children who hear hurtful words and are cut off by insensitive statements stop talking with and confiding in their parents. It is wise to consider as early as the one word stage how to pay attention to what children say. Verbal abuse and criticism from parents cause children to learn to hurt with words and to stop talking about deep and personal issues with their parents. "Don't talk and don't feel" become the rules children pick up on when parents' words sting and they do not take time to listen.

Toddlers do not talk about color even if well-meaning parents do. Parents notice color because they enjoy the variety and beauty of it. It does not move, jump, or bark. It is just not important for a one-word child to know about color until he is four or five years old, or unless he shows a particular interest in it earlier.

What we mean by "house," "nose" or "penny" is different than what the toddler means when he uses these kinds of words. Children discover the adult meaning of words through careful listening and observation of adult usage. "Dada" and "Mama" are common first words and parents feel so good when little ones begin to use them. But we may feel a twinge of alarm when our baby calls the man next door Dada. Remember at the one-word stage, a child uses a word in her own special way, which may not be the way Mom and Dad use it. One little girl used "Dada" to refer to the parent who played with her on the floor, whereas "Mama" was a call for help, to take care of needs and to provide comfort. Word meanings can be tricky, and it is hard to get them just right when you are only one-year old.

Children try to figure out how adults use words by listening to adults talk and trying to imitate them. For instance, in trying to figure out what the word "ball" means, toddlers often focus on roundness and mislabel objects like apples, oranges, balloons, and round doorknobs. This is an example of overextension where the word "ball" has come to mean small, round objects. "Dog" is often overextended to include cat, lamb, horse, cow or any other

42

furry, four-legged creature that runs around. It is not clear exactly how children come to use words in the same way that adults do. One idea with merit is that they learn more words that gradually take over the inappropriate overextension of their earlier words.

The one-word stage stimulates debate among researchers. Some people think that the first word a child produces has more than single-word meaning. The child intends to come out with a sentence, but cannot do it. First words may be attempts at stating complicated, sequential ideas. For example, a child hears and sees an airplane passing by, and calls out "airplane." :He tracks the airplane and then says "bye-bye". He probably means to say, "Look, there is an airplane, watch it go across the sky and now it has gone." But if you are a child and know only a few words, and have no idea of sentence structure, two unconnected words will have to do. At the end of the one-word stage it is common to hear a child utter one word, then stop, in a halting manner and say another word. One girl edged close to the two-word stage as she said "book" watching the book slip off the table, then, almost immediately, announced "down."

Children need to live with adults who talk to each other and to children in order to learn how to use language. The one word child eventually catches on that the words his parents utter are strung together in sequences. He is motivated to crack the code and figure out the trick to sequencing words. We call this sequencing grammar or syntax. A rich and interesting language world helps children to learn to speak and motivates them to want to use their language. Researchers have found that children use language in very different ways when they are alone, in comparison to when a parent engages them. Which situation do you think brings out advanced language for one-word toddlers: solitary play or play with Mom and Dad?

When Mom and Dad play games that are geared toward their child's interests and ability level, higher levels of language come out. Studies show that, children interacting with their parents used more new words, showed more willingness to try new words, have higher word counts for familiar words, use words more creatively, and use more expression and humor. When children play alone, with a peer or in a group of children, they use significantly less language, less complex language, and display less creativity.

One cold winter day, I had an idea that brightened up the next couple of dreary months. We got a box of large, soft plastic letters of the alphabet. They came in all different bright colors, both upper and lower case letters, and my boys, Ben and Kirk, then one-and-a-half and three-and-a-half years old, did not know what to do with them. That's when I came up with the idea of the game of Alphabet Town. On the playroom carpet, we used blocks to build many houses and stores, and we put trees and benches and cars all over Alphabet Town. Finally, one person hid a letter in or under each object. The two people who did not hide the letters were hiding their eyes, and when the letters were all hidden the other two players would find the letters and try to identify them. Many variations of this procedure evolved. Kirk loved this game because he was older and could remember many of the letters; Ben loved the game because he wanted to play with us and he liked letters at an early age. This is the way my children were exposed to letters of the alphabet, but more importantly, this is the way we spent afternoons constructing, rearranging, remembering, and talking. I got tired of the game within a few weeks, but we played it for two months until spring came. Once the trees were green and the flowers blooming, there were more interesting activities going on outside. Although the boys clearly know the alphabet now, I wonder if they remember how they learned it.

What can we conclude from this? It seems that parents encourage thinking. And, perhaps because it feels good to be with Mom and Dad, creative and humorous talk can take place easily. By and large, the motivation-thinking-feeling-talking cycle seems to take place in a more fluid and continuous way when young children are down on the floor close to Mom and Dad. As a matter of fact, because of the love and empathy that parents feel for their toddlers, they seem to be willing and able to go the extra mile. Researchers have noticed that parents keep up a kind of "joint attention" with their toddlers in play and talk that keeps the conversation going. Joint attention happens when an adult listens to what a child is saying, and joins in on his thoughts, feelings, and talk. Mom does not distract him with her own ideas; she stays with his ideas and gently builds upon them. When there is a lull, and he seems open to her input, she may add some ideas of her own. Researchers have looked for the effects of joint attention on parent-child conversations. They found that during episodes of joint attention both mothers and their children talked more, used shorter sentences, took more conversational turns, offered more comments, asked more questions and engaged in longer conversations. It seemed that when the mothers were able to initiate joint attention, the most tuned-in talking took place.

Joint attention is a skill that is useful beginning even before the one word-stage, and continuing through adolescence and adulthood. When parents can stay with their children's thoughts, feelings and talk, the child develops a secure sense of himself and keeps that feeling deep within him. So, much more than words is being communicated. It is not easy to jointly attend to an adolescent when he is struggling for his independence by pushing the parent away. However, he still needs reassurance and support.

Tomasello, M and Farrar, M.J. *Joint Attention and Early Language.* Child Development, 1986, vol 57(6), 1454-1463.

Sanford, Linda T. *Strong in the Broken Places.* Avon Books, New York, 1990.

Zukow, P.G. *The Relationship Between Interaction with the Caregiver and the Emergence of Play Activities During the One-Word Period.* 1986, vol 4(3), 223-234.

Wells, Gordon *Learning Through Interaction, The study of language development,* Cambridge University Press, Cambridge, 1981.

Chapter 4

Language Takes Off

"Not to let a word get in the way of its sentence, Nor to let a sentence get in the way of its intention, But to send your mind out to meet the intention as a guest: that is understanding."
-Fourth Century Chinese Proverb

Sam picked up a toy cupcake and said, "cookie," while two-year-old Leah looked on and suggested, "Mommy cupcake." Leah's mother was babysitting for Sam (age one and a half) and they were having a talk about toy food. Leah took the cupcake from Sam and gave it to her mother. "Eat cupcake," was Leah's next command as she watched in a self-satisfied manner while her mother pretended to eat. Sam exclaimed, "Eat," and laughed while Leah moved on to demand, "Leah eat," as she wrestled the cupcake from her mother. It is easy to see that Leah is the leader here: she can put two words together to make meaningful talk. She is two and a half years old.

When Leah puts two words together to make a sentence, she

is beginning to make words work for her. Leah is beginning to realize she can use talking to direct the conversation. When a child uses only one word, she shows that she can use symbols one at a time.

When she puts two words together, she shows that she can use symbols and she can combine symbols or words to make sentences. After a child combines two words with ease, her language improves dramatically.

Leah is motivated to interact and share her life with her parents and other people. Leah's thinking has flourished; her feelings are pure and natural. Put it all together, and Leah is like a missile launched and whizzing toward talk. When she talks, she can feel the power she possesses to start conversations. She will find she can initiate a myriad of conversations that help her grow and develop.

Leah has no idea why she said, "Leah eat," instead of, "Eat Leah." But it was not just a good guess. Leah, at age two, knows something about sentences. Every language has rules for making sentences, and every speaker knows the rules for his native language. We cannot list all the rules about how words go together, but we have implicit knowledge of how to do it. Leah is learning how to combine words and will do so swiftly and almost effortlessly by the time she is about three.

The language Leah can use now will help her work out problems and misunderstandings with her family. Leah's parents are ready to help her talk to express her needs. Just before Sam came to their house, Leah was busy taking a bath. She loves to splash and play until the end of the bath, when mother says it is time to shampoo her hair. When mother announced it was shampoo time, Leah asserted herself with an emphatic, "NO!"

Mother knew it was time for a talk. She asked Leah, "What do you mean? You do not want to shampoo now?"

Leah replied, "No now."

Mother questioned, "How about in two minutes? Then you can play for a while more."

After two minutes, Mother said it was now time to shampoo and Leah refused once again. Mother helped Leah put her feelings into words, "You do not like to shampoo, do you?"

Leah agreed and Mother encouraged her to say what upset her.

Leah responded, "Water eyes. Eyes (pointing to her closed eyes)." Leah did not like water in her eyes.

Mother told Leah, "That was good talking. You told me you do not like water in your eyes. (pause) Let's see. What can we do to help you?"

Leah pointed and replied, "Bunny there."

Mother looked and said, "Oh, you want your bunny towel. Maybe you can hold your towel up to your eyes when I shampoo your hair. Is that ok?"

Leah squeezed her bunny towel up to her eyes and Mother got busy.

This ordinary conversation is remarkable; a lot of thinking-feeling-talking was going on to solve the shampoo problem. Let's look at what happened. Leah had a strong feeling; she did not want a shampoo. At first, Mother thought that she just wanted a few more minutes to play , then Leah refused again, and it became clear the problem was bigger than that. Mother realized that Leah was afraid, and she wanted to find out what thoughts led to that feeling. She found out it scared Leah to have water in her eyes. Mother took on an attitude of, "What can we do together to solve the problem?" She wanted to collaborate with Leah and think together about what to do. She helped Leah get to the thought, "I am going to get water in my eyes," and she accepted the feeling, "I do not like shampoos." Then she intended to work on the solution to the problem by talking about it. That's when Leah came up with the idea to get the bunny towel. This is the thinking-feeling-talking cycle in action even in the two-word stage.

Notice that Mother wanted to know what upset Leah and work out the problem, but she was also able to insist on the need for a shampoo. To give in to Leah and postpone the shampoo would not be good for her because Leah cannot handle decisions on that scale yet. That is Mother's job.

A roomful of adults and children was sitting quietly at a prayer meeting. None of the children were allowed to eat the fruit and cookies on the table until the prayers were finished. A three year old girl insisted that she wanted to be allowed to eat before the twenty-minute meeting was over, but her parents explained that was not going to happen. The girl badgered her parents numerous times, and with only five minutes to go her father got up, gave her a cookie and ended her protests. But only for a short time.

Leah is learning about the big picture, the thinking-feeling-talking cycle while she is also learning on a smaller scale about individual words and sentences. She is making meaning by putting words together and learning about individual words and how to use them. A child begins to learn about word meaning toward the end of his first year of life. Leah, like Sam at age one-and-a-half, used the word "cookie" to mean cupcake. He also exclaimed "kitty" when he saw a rabbit, which meant that the word kitty included white, furry animals that move quickly. His use of the words "cookie" and "kitty" are broad and unrefined because he needs more experience and information about the world, which he gets by talking to his parents.

Each word contains a great deal of specific meaning. Leah knows a cupcake is not a cookie. When she uses a word she has to know what it means and how to use it in a sentence. Early on, word meaning was thought to be based on simple matching between objects and labels. People believed that each word had a physical counterpart in the world, and thus learning language was a matching game where you put things together with different sounds or words.

Theories of word meaning based on matching have been replaced by ideas of word meaning, where we make up categories for organizing what we see around us, based on our own particular way of thinking. People organize reality based on their perceptions and thoughts; there is no one to one correspondence with the physical world. A sweet, baked good with icing on top can be labeled cookie, biscuit, or cupcake depending on experience and culture. Words reflect our own special organization of the world. For instance, English speakers divide color into red and orange but this does not correspond to a natural division in physics or optics. The majority of words in any language divide reality in complex and subtle ways. This is why it is rare for two words to be exact synonyms. "That is a little boy" is different from "That is a small boy," yet the words little and small are synonyms. "Little" implies age in the first sentence and "small" implies size in the second.

This is important for parents to know because the way a child picks out a word and uses it reveals his thinking and feeling, and this helps us figure out how to talk to him. When a two year old calls a cupcake a "cookie", we can go on to model the word correctly, or we can gently remark that it does look like a cookie, but we call it a cupcake. For young children, word choice and thinking processes go hand in hand. At about eighteen months of age, just about the time the child will begin to put two words together, he begins to learn new words rapidly. About 14,000 words are learned between one year and five years which means that children are learning about nine new words a day. Parents find out what children think from what they say and do, then teach by example. Children need gentle, supportive models to help them use words and sentences the way adults do.

Subtle differences in word meaning make it difficult for a child (or an adult learner of a second language) to benefit fully from a dictionary. It is impossible to learn to speak from learning definitions. Children must have ample opportunity to hear new words and practice using new words. When a parent notices that his child is trying to express a thought or feeling, he can jump in and help him find the word or sentence. Words and phrases are learned from hearing good speakers; they are learned by reading good writers. Young children do not learn words by listening to long definitions from their parents, rather they learn words from hearing their parents use them in daily life.

Dad asked Leah what she wanted for her snack, and she said she wanted an apple. After washing the apple, Dad handed it to Leah, who then objected. She declared, "This off." paused and tried again, "Off Daddy." It took Dad a few moments but he finally got the idea that he was supposed to peel the apple. Dad told Leah they needed to find the scraper. Leah questioned, "Scraper, Daddy?" Dad got Leah up on a chair, and they looked for the scraper in a drawer full of utensils. It became a game, with Leah holding up a corkscrew and saying, "This scraper?" Dad patiently said, "No" and the search continued. Then Dad decided to play the game, so he held up various objects and asked Leah if each was the scraper. When they found the scraper, Leah had heard the word "scraper" several dozen times. It was her word now and the apple finally got peeled.

"Stir soup!" exclaimed Leah, as she stirred a ball around in her pan. But as Sam approached and grabbed the ball he informed her, "Ball," probably meaning, "That is a ball, it is not soup."

Sam is mobilizing some extraordinary and everyday developmental skills as he makes his correction. He first had to think about the difference between a ball and soup. Although he is limited by his one-word status, he experienced a feeling that he wanted to express. Somehow it was not acceptable to Sam that Leah was calling a ball "soup." The thought, "That is not a ball" preceded the feeling, "I feel bad when things are not labeled correctly." Talk comes next where Sam can use words to let Leah know about her mistake. Talk works for Sam to help him get his needs met and correct mistakes in his world.

When Leah put "stir and "soup" together she probably wanted to say, "I am stirring the soup," and her thought was probably, "I am pretending the ball is soup." But we do not really know if these are accurate translations, we can only guess. It is amazing that children put ideas together in predictable, developmental patterns. Some ideas are expressed by virtually all children learning to talk. Roger Brown, a psycholinguist, has found that more than

75 percent of children's two word sentences include predictable combinations. If you would like to get a lively conversation going with a two-year-old below are some ideas. Parents can use these examples and form their sentences based on these two-word combinations to help their children learn these patterns. Mom can nudge Sam ahead by helping him say, "That is a ball." as in Number 1 below. She can follow up for him by saying, "That is not soup." which is negation (number 9 below).

1.	Naming	that and noun	that apple
2.	Noticing	hi and noun	hi kitty
3.	Getting more	another and noun	more juice
4.	Disappearing	all gone and noun (or ending)	all gone ball
5.	Describing	adjective and noun	big noise
6.	Possessing	noun and noun	mommy cookie
7.	Action	verb and noun	stir tea
8.	Locating	noun and noun	hat chair
9.	Negation	verb and noun	not soup
10.	Person-action	noun and verb	Ben eat
11.	Person-object	noun and noun	Daddy book
12.	Action-object	verb and noun	sit chair
13.	Naming	that and noun	that apple
14.	Noticing	hi and noun	hi kitty
15.	Getting more	another and noun	more juice
16.	Disappearing	all gone and noun	all gone ball

Looking at the above list clues us into what children can do with just two words. Leah said, "Stir soup," which is number 7 action. This list also gives us a glimpse of some feelings and needs; children need to express getting more, disappearing and possession among other ideas. How can we as parents help them with this? The thinking-feeling-talking idea can give us some suggestions for getting two-year-old conversations going. Whatever a two-year-old does is based on two-year-old thinking and likewise for three-year-olds, four-year-olds, and sixteen-year-olds. It is fine to think like people in your age range. If a two-year-old like Sam notices a contradiction in his way of thinking, he feels something about it. This feeling is also fine. It does not give him the right to throw the ball at Leah or grab the pan. But his feelings will match his thoughts. This is a clue for parents to use to know when to step in. Put your efforts into helping him to change his thinking, and his feelings will fall into place.

I do not mean to belabor Sam's one small word "ball" but it is a handy example to use to show how Mom can help Sam. Mom can help Sam to think of a ball as being pretend soup.

Mom: Sam, Leah wants soup. Where is soup?
Sam: Dere. (points toward kitchen)
Mom: That soup is for Mommy.
Sam: Leah.
Mom: I cannot give it to Leah. The soup is for supper.
Sam: Sam.
Mom: Yes, the soup is for Sam's supper. Leah wants to play. (pause) What can she use to play?
Sam: (gets a toy pan)
Mom: Want to use this paper? (tears up small pieces of paper to use as soup)
Sam: Soup?
Mom: Yes, pretend this is soup.
Sam: (stirs the soup)
Mom: Or we can use a ball like Leah did.

It is clear that Mom helped Sam to understand how paper or a ball can represent soup. Once Sam began to understand "pretending" he felt better about using one object to stand for another object. Change the thinking through talk and demonstration; then the feelings will fall into place.

Leah does not want to get into her car seat. She doesn't hold back, she just says, "No." Dad acknowledges that she does not like her car seat, but explains that she must ride in her seat because it is safe and they have to go shopping now. Leah points to her Dad's seat and takes a chance, "Big seat?" while Dad explains once again, "No, you have to ride in your own car seat." Leah protests loudly as Dad lifts her into her seat. Dad leans over her and says, "If you sit in your seat quietly, I will tell you a story as we go." After further protest Leah opts for negotiation and says, "Kitty book." Then she sits quietly and waits for the story.

Again we can see that once Leah comes to the thought, "Dad is not going to give in. I have to sit in my car seat," she can change her feelings to, "Ok, he is going to win this one and I can accept that because he is offering me a story." When we help children to think the situation through, they have a good chance of smoothing out feelings too.

Brown, Roger *A First Language: The Early Stages.* Harvard University Press, Cambridge, MA, 1973.

Dale, Phillip S. *Language Development: Structure and Function.* Holt, Rinehart and Winston, 1976.

Chapter 5

Teach Me To Talk To You, Baby!

"Learning to communicate is a collaborative affair....the abilities that the child develops to understand and control the world in which he lives will owe much to... interpersonal collaboration."

Gordon Wells

Sophie, a two-year-old child, sat with her legs crossed, flipping through the pages of a magazine. It was a nature magazine and Sophie saw a picture of a tiger. "Daddy, see dis tiger!" Sophie exclaimed as she tried to get her father excited too. Sophie's father put his newspaper down to give her his attention and discuss the tiger. Sophie began to tell a wild tale of what was happening in the picture. Her father listened and marveled at her imaginative story. Sophie's father was as interested in her enthusiasm and her language as he was in her tiger story.

Parents are assistants in the child's process of motivation-thinking-feeling-talking. The world and language stimulate children's minds. They are so good at thinking and talking that they are willing and able to drag their parents along. Children set up ground rules for what they need from their parents to become motivated, think, feel and talk. They need parental input but realize it has to be packaged especially for them. Parents use language to move the child gently to higher levels of thinking and learning. Meanwhile, children respond to talk that makes sense to them, and let parents know what is beyond them. And so children and parents go back and forth with this kind of reaching and stretching.

Judy was a cute and confident three-year-old when she and her mother had the following conversation.

Judy: I don't want to go out today.
Mother: Why? Wouldn't you like to play in the yard? It is
          such a warm, sunny day today.
Judy: No, I can't go out in the yard.
Mother: You usually like to play in your sandbox and on your
          swings. What is the matter?
Judy: Sunshine.
Mother: But sunshine won't hurt you. We could put some sun-
          screen on if you are worried.
Judy: No, sunshine bites kids even if they have sunscreen
          on.

No one knows exactly how the entire language process develops, but we do know a few important strategies for learning to talk. We understand that communication is a motivation-thinking-feeling-talking process that comes out of many daily interactions between children and caring adults. Researchers have studied moms and dads (mostly moms) to try to understand what adults do that encourages children to talk. They listened to children speaking in ways that adults imitate. The language parents use with their children is different from other talk. Parents' words to a one-year-old are different from words used with a ten-year-old. Thus, parents vary their language based on whether they are speaking to an adult or a child. Parents get to know their own children so well that they can fine-tune their talk to meet the children's needs. Adjustments on both sides are part of it all.

As an example of this mutual feedback, let's observe Sophie and her Mom together. Sophie loved to do puzzles with her mother and from an early age, puzzles fascinated her. When Sophie was two, they would have conversations like this:

Mom: Look, Sophie, here is a piece of Donald Duck's head. Where do you think we should put it?

Sophie: Down here.

Mom: But down there is where his feet go.

Sophie: Oh, here? (Up at top on right)

Mom: Yes, up here at the top. But look at the picture of the puzzle we are doing. (Shows her the box cover) On this side, the right side, we see who? Who is that?

Sophie: The baby duck.

Mom: Yes, one of the baby ducks goes on this side. So on which side should we put Donald Duck?

Sophie: This side. (Points to left)

Mom: Yes, great job!

Mom stays with Sophie. She helps to look at the puzzle for clues for where to put the pieces. When Sophie does not know for sure what to do, she tries. Her effort prompts her mother to help her.

One strategy parents learn early is to be one step ahead of their language-learning child. Mom and Dad should not stay on the same learning level as their child. They should aim for one small notch above. Parents challenge children by keeping their talk ahead to prod them along to higher levels. As an example, consider Jake and his mother making sand castles at the beach.

Mom: Look at those great sandcastles!
Jake: (age three): I want one.
Mom: Which one do you want?
Jake: This. (he points)
Mom: This big one? Do you want to make this big sandcastle?
Jake: Yes, the big one.
Mom: Ok. Which pail should we use to make the big sandcastle?
Jake: Don't know.
Mom: If you want a big sandcastle, then you use the big pail. Which is the big pail?
Jake: This is big.
Mom: Yes it is. But go put it right up to that sandcastle. Which is bigger? The pail or the castle?
Jake: The castle is bigger.
Mom: So what do we need?
Jake: The real big pail.

Mom keeps her talk short, but her conversation is always longer and more complicated than Jake's. How do moms do this? To simplify their speech they use shorter sentences than when they talk to adults. They speak more clearly and more slowly. Parents know how to use fewer verbs (jump, run, speak), fewer adjectives (red, smooth, drippy), and fewer prepositions (under, over, on). Parents speak in the present tense (what is happening now), and their choice of words is simple and clear. Parents are willing to say the same phrases repeatedly for the child's sake. They know how to ask many questions to encourage the child to understand and focus on the main points. Over sixty percent of parent-talk to children involves questions. How many questions did Mom have to ask Jake to get him to choose the big pail?

Parents simplify their talk at each level of language development. Remember that Sophie is two. Sophie's mother helped her take the top off a pan, and tried to get Sophie to talk. Sophie understands her mother's sentences though she cannot produce them. Yet, Sophie picks out key words and uses those to stay with the conversation.

Mother:	Can you take the top off?
Sophie:	Off. (child looks at pan)
Mother:	See the handle? (points to handle)
Sophie :	Handle? (touches handle, looks at mother)
Mother:	See? The top is off. (mother takes top off)
Sophie :	Sophie takes top off. (Sophie takes top off and laughs)
Mother:	Good Sophie! You took the top off the pan.

Mothers talked into a tape recorder to pretend to have a conversation with a two-year-old child. Notice the word "pretend." Some researchers were trying to compare tape-recorded language to the way mothers actually talked to their two-year-old. Moms failed. It was hard for them to simplify their talk without real children to provide the right cues. The taped mother-talk was not at all as simplified as real mother-talk. This surprising result shows that mothers take their cues from their children. This means that children give their parents tips on what to say and how to say it. Mother and the child listen carefully to one another and make their talk dependent on what the other says. Mother depends on the child's responses, like the child depends on hers.

Language simplification is not something that parents know much about before having children. The ability comes from contact with children, with empathy for them. Because parents love and feel for their children, they adjust what they say so their children can understand and benefit. Parents watch their children, listen to their children and form a composite memory of each child's skill level. This composite memory serves as a guide that helps make their talk match the child's level. Adults who do not have young children tend not to simplify their language in the presence of children. Adults without children do not have a composite memory of what a child at age three can say and do. Adults with young children adjust their talk to the level of any new child.

Here is an irony. Parents are simplifying their talk to children. They are making their words simple, but not too simple. Parents do not talk exactly at their child's level; they make it tougher for their child. A parent can gauge a child's level of understanding and nudge the child a bit higher all in one motion.

A toddler says, "kitty" and mother repeats, "Yes, there's a kitty." The child says, "Meow" and mother fills in with, "Yes, the kitty says meow." This is an example of how mothers imitate children's words exactly (she repeats "kitty" and "meow"), but she also expands upon the child's words. Parents look for clues on how to fill in missing words. They look around to see what the child could have seen. Parents rely on social context for clues. They watch what the child is doing, and remember what he likes. They use all this knowledge to guess what the child intended to say. This adding on is the way children move up, notch by notch, in their learning. It is called "expansion," and here are two examples of expansion with Mom and Sophie (age two):

I.

Mother:	Here is toast for you.
Sophie:	Sophie toast.
Mother:	Yes, that is your toast.
Sophie:	Mama toast.
Mother:	Yes, I eat my toast. (Pause) Do you want to eat toast?
Sophie:	Eat Mama toast.
Mother:	You want Mamma's toast?
Sophie:	Yeah.
Mother:	My toast tastes better than yours?
Sophie:	No, mine better.

II.

Sophie:	Doggie.
Mother:	See the doggie.
Sophie:	Doggie run. (Points to dog)
Mother:	Yes, he runs fast.
Sophie:	Come doggie. Come here.
Mother:	Do you want to call the dog?

Sophie: (Nods)
Mother: Call him. Say, "come here dog!"
Sophie: Come here. (Tries again) Come here, Spotty.
Mother: His name is Spotty?

Not only do parents learn to expand children's talk but they match their talk to the child's topic. In the above example, the mother matches her comments about the dog to Sophie's words. She tries to understand her thinking and carry it forward one step. She does introduce another topic without Sophie's participation. The mother stays with her child's idea and expands upon it. Then she waits for the child's next comment. Many studies have shown that children benefit tremendously from the parent's ability to match topics and maintain joint attention. This is extremely important for children to learn how to stay on a topic and follow it through to completion. It feels satisfying for any person to have someone listen.

An old fashioned theory went like this: Mom and Dad say the words and sentences, kids repeat them. Long ago people thought that language acquisition was simply a matter of imitation; the child says what he hears. With some practice the child's mimicking improves and his parents provide reinforcement or rewards to correct mistakes. Children do use the same sounds, words and grammar, as do adults. They rarely repeat what they hear verbatim. Language acquisition is a creative process. When children speak their first words, the meaning and sound have little resemblance to adult use. Children figure out how to make sounds and use words slowly in small steps. As their knowledge of the world grows, their use of words becomes more exact.

Mothers imitate children's words more than children imitate adults'. For example, a toddler says, "Juice?" and mother responds, "Yes, juice." Consider this example, a toddler says "Kitty" and mother repeats "Yes, there's a kitty." Young children do far less imitating in their language learning than was once thought. Instead, it turns out that children do more problem solving and detective work to learn to talk. Children hear sounds and words, and they think about what they mean and how to put them together. Baby talk is imaginative. Children are thinkers, not parrots. Thinking and feeling are the key ingredients necessary for learning how to talk. Children use words in a variety of novel ways that show mental work instead of blind imitation.

Sophie learned the phrase "polka dot". She loved the polka dots on her mother's blouse. In a clothing store, she insisted her mother buy her a polka dot dress. Then Grandpa came to visit. While Sophie played on Grandpa's lap, she stared at his nose. She exclaimed, "Grampa, got polka dot nose." Sophie knew how to use the word and apply it, creatively, to new situations.

Dale, Philip, S. *Language Development: Structure and Function*. Holt, Rhinehart and Winston, New York, 1976.

Furrow, David and Nelson Katherine *A Further Look at the Motherese Hypothesis*: a reply to Gleitman, Newport and Gleitman. Journal of Child Language, 13, 163-176, 1986.

Rice, Mabel L. *Children's Language Acquisition*. American Psychologist, 44(2), 1989.

Wells, Gordon *Learning Through Interaction*. Cambridge University Press, 1981.

Chapter 6

People-Talk

"The function of language is to portray the mysteries and secrets of human hearts." Abd'u'lBaha

Once a baby can talk, he can speak about objects and people. As he grows, he can use language to explore computers, aviation, philosophy, culinary arts, and nuclear physics. He can use language to cultivate friendships, build a healthy family, and participate in community affairs. Language, in the first list, is for thinking while language, in the second, involves relationships with people. People-talk is speech that is intended to reach people.

Conversation is collaborative; it takes at least two to converse. Each person takes a turn and then stops for the next person. Most adults can time their speaking turn to begin within milliseconds of the time at which the other speaker stops. There are long gaps between young children's speaking turns, but as children reach six or seven, their timing in conversation becomes more like adults.

In any conversation, there is a speaker who sends a message, and a listener who tries to understand the message. There is also a situation or setting in which the speaking takes place. The setting includes people, location, and mood or tone. We take our behavioral cues from the setting. Think about how you would act and talk if you were in a church, a football stadium, or at a rocket-launch.

Children learn early how to consider the social setting when deciding what to say. Below is a conversation my son and I had when he was five. At first, it might seem Ben was simply asking for permission to go out of the yard, but he had an ulterior motive.

Ben: Mom, can Kevin and I play down in the neighbor-hood?

Mother: Why are you asking me that? You know the rule. When you have a friend over to play you have to stay in our yard.

Ben: I know, but I just wanted to ask.

Mother: Why?

Ben: (shrugs and smiles)

Mother: Did you want Kevin to know that you play down in the neighborhood by yourself sometimes?

Ben: (nods yes)

Mother: Well, you are quite a big boy now. But play in our yard today because Kevin is here.

Five-year-old children realize questions can be used for purposes other than requesting. Questions can be used to show how much freedom one has earned.

When a child says, "ball" in order to induce his mother to throw the ball, he is arranging the social setting. When he says, "Come on," and pulls his father's hand, he is influencing people. Children get their needs met using people even in the two-word stage. They can say, "Mama cup," "Kitty there," or "Dada peas," to make a change in the social context. They direct our attention, refocus our topics, and even tell us what to eat.

When we talk to children, we teach them how to use words and have relationships with people. For what purpose?

The answer is that communication is the key to being with

people. Getting along with people means success in family, school, and work. The more children know about language and how to use it, the more effective they are.

On rare occasions, children have trouble with language development and do not respond to their parents' attempts to talk to them. When I first met John he was three years old with dark black hair, a round face, and a little turned up nose. He stared into space. Marie, John's mother, would say, "The car is going down the road," as she moved his toy car across the living room carpet. John would say, "The blue car goes fast," as he pushed his car across some blocks. Then Marie would say, "The red car is going up the driveway," and John might add, "There are cars in the driveway."

If Marie asked, "Where are the cars, John?" John would stare across the room. Then Marie would try again, "Can you make your car go zoooommmm like this?" John would remain motionless and gaze at the wall.

John could not answer questions. He could not follow directions, nor could he repeat words. He could not use the language he knew to connect with a human being. John could speak when he was next to his mother. When she spoke to him, he fell silent. He could talk if his words were about objects set apart from people. John did not respond directly to his mother's talk or actions. He could not make his own words and ideas correspond to any social setting. Speaking words and communicating with people are two aspects of talking that are, under normal circumstances, inseparable.

Psychiatrists determined that John was not autistic, or psychotic. John had an unusual kind of attention deficit disorder and learning disability. He found social information to be overwhelming and incomprehensible. To "Pick up the doll," John would become confused and stand motionless, as if frozen. The thinking-feeling- talking cycle helps to understand John.

THOUGHTS JOHN MAY HAVE HAD
1. I don't understand what she is saying.
2. I don't know why she is talking to me.
3. She seems to want me to do something but I do not know what to do.

FEELINGS JOHN MAY HAVE HAD
1. I feel sad and left out and all alone.
2. I feel confused and frustrated.
3. I feel angry and I am not sure what to do.

JOHN'S TALKING
1. Mom says, "I am putting my ball here."
   John says, "This ball is green."
2. Mom says, "I am driving my car to the garage."
   John says, "Here is the wheel."
3. Mom says, "Would you like a cookie?"
   John says nothing, but stares at the couch blankly.

John's mother had been trying to get John to talk to her since he was a baby. Marie showed persistence in continuing to talk to John, though he would not reply. John was attached to Marie, he loved to be close to her. Marie was patient and understanding with him. Her efforts to reach him were not without reward. John listened when his mother spoke because he learned vocabulary and syntax. Here is an excerpt of an article written about John.

"John appeared to possess a set of highly specialized language-based routines which were tied to specific situations. If the toy that was eliciting the language was removed, John stopped speaking and might then move around his house silently or only occasionally uttering a comment for periods as long as one or two hours. If another toy was then introduced by the parents, he would be drawn into the situation and begin to use the verbal routines associated with that toy. Again, should that toy be removed, silence would ensue. Furthermore, the lexicon produced in the initial learning of any one play sequence was rarely used in any other setting (e.g. although he would talk about cars in the car game, when he was actually driving in a car, John did not discuss the objects that now were before him.) It seems therefore that John's language both developed and was used in what can best be described as symbolic play situations. It rarely appeared in the more typical ways that are characteristic of young children's initial language development such as requests to meet demands ("more cookie"), gain attention ("hi there") or assert independence ("me do it")."

Children figure out what to say and how to say it based on different settings. The social context of language was confusing for John. John learned to speak from play rituals but he could not communicate with the words he knew. He attended a special school where he received education and therapy. He made progress slowly and began to learn how to use language with people. Communication was broken down into small parts and taught to John in steps. Most children learn people-talk naturally and easily. For John, it is a monumental effort.

Blank, M., Gessner, M. and Esposito (Remig), A. *Language Without Communication: A Case Study.* Journal of Child Language, 1979.

Garvey, Catherine *Children's Talk.* Cambridge University Press, 1984.

Wells, Gordon *Learning Through Interaction: The Study of Language Interaction.* Cambridge University Press, 1981

Chapter 7

Getting Ready for School?

"What I want to suggest is that stories have a role in education that goes far beyond their contribution to the acquisition of literacy. Constructing stories... pervades all of learning."

-Gordon Wells

Before your baby is born, you are getting him ready for school. You talked to him and sang to him. He heard a variety of stimulating sounds. Julie, Sam, Sophie, and Leah and all the children mentioned are prepared for school. Their parents talked to them and taught them to be good communicators. The ability to speak and have a conversation is the first step in school success. The most powerful tool parents use to get their children ready for school is conversation.

Picture a child deprived of a rich and rewarding language environment. This child has not heard adults converse intelligently. He has not learned how to combine thoughts into sensible statements, describe feelings with clarity, and organize his impressions of events into a coherent story. He has not gotten the healthy and stimulating communication he needed from his parents or from a preschool program. Picture what will happen to him when he starts school. He will be behind before he even walks through the door. Parents' words to children are food for their brains.

The second step in getting ready for school is familiarity with storybooks. Gordon Wells, a psycholinguist, has shown that children whose parents read them stories, from before they could talk, and are read to through elementary school, are children who do well in school.

Wells writes:

There are many ways in which parents foster their children's development in these (early) years, not least through the quality of their conversation with them. But what this study clearly demonstrates is that it is growing up in a literate family environment, in which reading and writing are naturally occurring, daily activities, that gives children a particular advantage when they start their formal education. And of all the activities that were characteristic of such homes, it was the sharing of stories that we found to be the most important (p. 194).

The effect of storybooks on children is miraculous. Stories set the child's mind in motion. Stories have a beginning, middle, and an end. We remember the parts of the story in order to understand it. A story organizes information into a coordinated sequence. This is food for the child's mind. Nancy Larrick writes, "Innumerable research studies arrive at the same conclusion; five year olds who have been read to continuously (throughout their young life) speak with confidence and seek answers to questions. Often they are ready to plunge into independent reading. In fact, some are already reading on their own (p. 3)."

All schoolwork is based on the idea of a story. When Joe

comes running home from third grade saying he has to do a project on frogs, he is light years ahead if he knows about stories. In essence, he has been asked to tell the story of how an egg laid by a female frog is fertilized, grows into a tadpole, and develops limb by limb into a frog. Psycholinguists believe that the storybooks read to young children are the prototype of all knowledge that exists in the world. All theories in science are logical sequences of ideas proposed to explain the world of nature. The format of a story, whether it is in a book on nuclear physics or Grimms Fairy Tales, has a beginning, a middle, and an end tied together by logical connections.

Not only is reading stories brain food, children enjoy being close to their parents while reading. Sharing books is an activity that is enjoyable for a child from the first year of life on through the preadolescent years. The mother or father who reads with his or her child regularly not only spends quality time with that child, but raises a youngster with good language skills and a love for reading.

"Family storybook reading is a time when parents and children create their own special kind of magic. Whatever happens during the day, sharing storybooks brings the family together. Just a few minutes into the book and busy schedules are left behind, accidents are forgotten, and bad tempers fade" (Taylor and Strickland, p. 3).

Children with average or above language skills benefit from hearing the words of a book. Children with less than average language ability or with learning disabilities sometimes fail to understand, and lose interest. Language problems cause the slow learner to feel bored, and thus he receives less exposure to language and reading. This becomes a vicious cycle and he falls behind.

Sue was an elementary school teacher who read stories in a way that mesmerized children. She was an actor, a mime, an educator, a counselor, and a linguist. She got even the most language-shy youngsters to become part of the excitement. She used the author's words and interjected her own. She encouraged reticent children to try to guess what would happen next. Active participation was the key Sue used to stimulate language production in children as they listened and comprehended.

1. Sue (reading a book to her first grade class): Look at the cover of this book. Who do you think we will read about today?

   Children: Red Riding Hood

2. Sue: Yes, very good. Did we read about a character like her recently? Anybody remember another girl in a story?

   Children: Goldie Locks.

3. Sue: Tell me what is the same about Red Riding Hood and Goldie Locks.

   Children: They are girls, they wear dresses, they have families.

4. Sue: Great. Now there are characters in this story who are not on the cover, think of them.

   Children: The wolf!

5. Sue: Yes, the wolf will show up later. How do you feel about him? Would you like to meet him?

   Children: Yes! No!

6. Sue (begins to read): What time of day is it here? Is Red Riding Hood going to bed?

Reading storybooks is an active process. Parents ask questions and make comments that seem natural to the story line. Studies have shown that preschool children may not follow the story line of a book. They may not even realize the pages of a book are related to each other. When parents take the time to explain story lines and plots to the child, then he understands sequential ideas better. Children begin to understand that books have continuous and progressive themes the more they read. The coordination of separate ideas is encouraged and the child begins to understand that a book is the gradual unfolding of a complicated pattern. The more he reads the more confident he gets that he can figure out the patterns or plots of books. Can you match Sue's questions with this list?

Simple Naming

Children in the first and second years of life like to name objects. Sometimes the parent says, "What's that?" to each picture and the child delights in labeling familiar things. Children at this age like to hear and learn animal noises such as, "What does the kitty say?"

Completing a Sentence

Toward the end of the second year children are able to finish a sentence. The parent says, "The kitty likes to drink ******."

Memory

Immediate memory items are the easiest for children. Dad points to an apple in the book, then covers it up with his hand. He asks the child to tell him what picture is under his hand.

Ask for some long-term memories such as, "Can you tell me about the story we just read?" "Can you remember the one we read yesterday about Henny Penny?"

Describing An Event

"What's happening in this picture?" can be a tough question for a young child. He has to look at the picture and try and figure out what is going on. Often knowing the story helps the child to explain what is happening.

Action Questions

Children love action and movement. Parents can ask, "What is the girl doing?" If the girl in the book rides her bike, then the children pretend to ride. When the boy climbs a tree, the children climb a pretend tree.

Attribute Questions

How do we help a child become aware of shapes, sizes, contours, distance and all kinds of different attributes? Find words to describe things. "Look at this giant's beard. What do you think it feels like?"

Spatial Questions

Children like to point to all the areas around them. Help them to understand words like: next to, on top of, up high, in front, around the corner, underneath.

Exclusion Questions

Children think about what is in front of them and what they can see. To extend their thinking, we ask them to imagine something they do not see on a page. Or we ask them to look at this boy and tell us what he has not put on.

Time Questions

Children learn to tell time by about eight-years-old, although they will learn faster with practice. Here are some time questions: Who came into the room first? Who finished eating last? Which mittens were dirty first? Who will win the race, and who will come in last? How long did it take for Little Red Riding Hood to get to her grandmother's house?

Difference Questions

Knowing what is different about two dolls is easier than knowing what is the same. Differences stand out in our mind and we notice them. A Raggedy Ann doll is softer than a plastic doll. You can ask what's different about balls, trees, books, houses, or people.

Similarity Questions

It is harder to figure out "What is the same?" compared to "What is different?" Similarities do not catch our attention. When a child looks at a picture of a racing car and a station wagon, he will easily see that the two cars are different. We can help him see the similarities too: they both go fast, have wheels and brakes, and use gasoline to go. Do they have headlights? How do you get into the cars? Where would you store packages?

Feeling Questions

Children need to learn about feelings. No one is born understanding their own feelings or other people's. What did the rabbit feel as the fox chased him into the log? Why does brother mouse want a new baby mouse? Practice identifying feelings: sad, mad, bad, glad, and sacred. Look at what thoughts led to feelings.

Tina remained quiet. She would not talk in class and would only communicate with a couple of friends. Her parents did not talk to her individually. She did not try her own thinking out and express herself. Her lack of confidence caused her to become non-communicative when the teacher tried to talk to her. Tina did not bother to try in classroom or standardized tests; she just randomly filled in answers. Tina fell behind in school, and was placed in the lowest of eight sections.

Tina could not talk, nor could she take tests. But this did not mean that she did not learn. She learned enough to have this conversation take place. Tina, twelve, was talking to her English teacher. He was confused, and told her so as he handed back a paper.

Teacher:	Tina, I read your paper and I am afraid that you did not write this. I am worried that someone else wrote this. You know that is wrong and we call it plagiarism.
Tina:	(too frightened to talk—nods head)
Teacher:	I am afraid that you will have to stay after school and write another story. I cannot accept this story because you did not write it.
Tina:	(stares at him blankly)
Teacher:	Now you sit here and write while I will work at my desk. You cannot leave until your paper is finished.

Tina: (nods yes and begins to work; after forty-five minutes brings the paper up to Mr. Stewart.)

Teacher: Thank you, Tina. I will read it now. (he reads it) Why Tina this is a continuation of the other story on autumn. This is a good story too! This is well written! Tina, you wrote both stories? Why didn't you tell me?

Tina: (shrugs)

Teacher: Tina, why don't you talk to me?

Tina: I don't know.

Teacher: I want to talk to you. I will not get mad at you anymore. I am sorry. I can see that you did write the first story and now this one. Tell me why you did not speak?

Tina: I did not know what to say. I thought you would be angry and yell at me if I said anything.

Teacher: I would not have been angry with you but I would have asked you to write this other story anyway. I see that this was my mistake.

Tina worked with her teacher. He did not give her answers, he just encouraged her to try and talked to her. Within a few days, Tina was moved up to one of the top groups in the school to study with classmates that she would be with until high school graduation. She was graduated from high school with good grades and went on to perform well in college. Tina's inability to talk and the distraction caused by her emotional problems left her incapable until Mr. Stewart noticed her ability and encouraged her.

Blank, Marion *Language, the Child, and the Teacher: A Proposed Assessment Model. Psychological Processes in Early Education,* Academic Press, New York, 1976.

Larrick, Nancy *A Parent's Guide to Children's Reading.* The Westminster Press, Philadelphia, 1982.

Taylor, Dennis and Strickland, Dorothy S. *Family Storybook Reading,* Heinemann Educational Books, Inc., New Hampshire, 1986.

Wells, Gordon   *The Meaning Makers.* Heinemann Educational Books, Inc. Portsmouth, N.H., 1986.

SECTION II
FAMILY BUILDING

"The communion that can be achieved by human conversation is of great significance for our private lives. It unites the members of a family—husbands and wives, parents and children. It is the spiritual parallel of the physical union by which lovers try to become one.

Please note that I did not say, 'the communion achieved by human conversation.' I said rather 'the communication that can be achieved by human conversation.' Human beings sometimes—in fact, too often—fail to achieve it by their failures as speakers and listeners in two-way talk, especially in personal heart-to-heart talks."

-Mortimer J. Adler

Chapter 8

Family Language

"Those who forget the past are always destined to repeat it."

-Santayana

The words we choose to describe families and children reflect our feelings about them. Do you remember this old nursery rhyme?

There was an old woman
Who lived in a shoe
She had so many children
She didn't know what to do.
She gave them some broth
Without any bread
Whipped them all soundly
And sent them to bed.

A different version of "The Old Woman Who Lived in a Shoe" was published in 1947 by Rand McNally and Company. This contrasting version of the rhyme gives an entirely different impression of the old woman and her family.

There was an old woman
Who lived in a shoe
She had so many children
She didn't know what to do.
But they were all so handsome
And clever, I'm told
That she wouldn't trade one
For diamonds or gold.

Children, as well as adults, listen to the words they hear from loved ones, and as a result they develop ideas and feelings about family life. Negative language about children, parents, and families has an impact on children. The way parents choose to speak to their children affects the children emotionally, spiritually, socially, and even physically. Children will come to understand who they are by the way their parents speak to them.

From infancy through adolescence, interaction between parents and children is critical for language learning. Self-knowledge begins with the child's understanding of his parents' words to him. If he is called lazy, he will believe he is lazy. Parents' language, and the feeling conveyed with it, will affect how the child feels about himself and this will be the basis of his self-esteem. The child who is called lazy realizes that being lazy is reprehensible and his self-esteem will diminish.

As adults, we use some of the same words that we heard our parents use. Certain phrases and expressions are repeated in families so frequently that the children continue to use the same words. This is fine if the language is descriptive, humorous, or endearing. If the words being passed on are offensive, it is difficult to forget and even harder to stop feeling. Sometimes we use words from our childhood reflexively. One mother did not believe it was right to spank her children. She had heard the phrase "Do you want a spanking?" often in her childhood and sometimes blurted it out with her own children.

Parents develop language styles early in life, and these styles inevitably have an effect on their children. Each language style described below has an effect on children, but the effect appears to differ for individual children. Resilient children will be influenced differently than sensitive children.

Most people fall into one of several patterns of communication. Communicative styles are alterable. People cannot accurately judge how their communication affects others. Understanding one's own communicative style requires self-observation and self-monitoring in combination with soliciting the opinions of trusted people.

Four common communication styles are presented: the loquacious talker, the depressed talker, the passive talker, and the angry talker. All are seen in both men and women, although certain styles may be more typical of one sex. Women tend to be more loquacious and more passive in their communication. Each parent brings to his child rearing the experiences and communication history of his own early life. These influences, with his own personality, will produce a child's own unique communication style.

The Loquacious Communicator

"...Observe silence and refrain from idle talk. For the tongue is a smoldering fire, and excess of speech a deadly poison." (Baha'u'llah)

The loquacious person talks too much. The topic typically concerns his own feelings, views, and needs. He uses words to explore meaning in his own life, and has a strong need to express his feelings. The loquacious talker provides an abundant language environment for the child. The child hears a great deal of language. The child is exposed to more language than he can benefit from. The child learns that language is overwhelming. The function of talk is seen by the child as self-serving. Although the child does hear talk that he can respond to at times, he learns he cannot respond to most of it. The talk is not adjusted to the child's level of comprehension because most of it is not spoken for the child's sake. He has little opportunity to express himself.

The child may perceive that the loquacious parent takes more and longer turns. The child will eventually observe his parent talking too much with other family members and friends. The obvious imbalance will cause the child some concern no matter how he chooses to resolve his feelings. A sensitive child may withdraw from the verbal barrage. Underneath, there will be some resentment, because each person wants to be heard. A child who is unable to share openly and intimately with his parent at times, will feel left out and unimportant.

Some children are assertive. They seize their conversational turns. Outspoken children find a way to be heard in spite of a loquacious parent. These children often model their loquacious parent and adopt a similar talkative style. The child will not be aware that loquacity does not lend itself open communication.

I believe the motivation-thinking-feeling-talking idea can help us improve our communication with other people and alter our own self-talk. First comes our motivation to learn healthy communication. Remember thoughts come before feelings.

Helpful Thoughts on Talking

1. If I do not talk now those people may look down on me or think less of me. They expect me to talk, but I am going to consider whether I want to say something or I am feeling pressured to talk. I have to hold up my end of the conversation, not the whole conversation. It is ok for me to have time to think. Someone else can speak or we can have some silence.

2. It is ok for me to go unnoticed. I do not have the obligation to entertain and amuse people. I can be accepted and valued when I am not in the middle of the conversation.

3. I may not have to express this feeling inside. Let me try to listen. I can find other ways to calm and comfort myself.

4. Other people may want to know what I am thinking, but they probably want to express their own thoughts as much as they want to listen. I would like to share my observations and experiences but I can do so in my own time, when there is a natural pause.

The Passive Communicator

The passive communicator hesitates to talk, and his child often does not get enough conversation. The child does not enjoy the free-flowing give and take of conversation. Each child needs help to process the events going on around him and to be actively engaged in communication.

The passive communicator may not defend the child verbally. There are times in every child's life when a parent must speak up for him either to a friend, teacher, or other family member. There are clearly times in every child's life when one parent must speak up for the child to the other parent. Mothers or fathers who are afraid to defend their children place them in jeopardy. The passive parent may be unable to verbally protect the child.

There are different reasons for passivity and reticence. Lack of confidence contributes to passivity. A mother who is unsure of herself is less inclined to act on behalf of her child. A passive father has learned that withdrawal is safe and easy. The child is sacrificed for the desire to be safe and fend off conflict. Reticence also comes from fear. Some parents have learned to fear other people or the other parent and are incapable of routine comments that make conversation more fair. Equitable and just treatment can only be achieved in families through open communication.

Helpful Thoughts about Passivity

1. I have been criticized before, but so has every other human being on earth. Benjamin Franklin said we can all count on death and taxes, but I would like to add criticism to that list. When we stop and think about it, we have all lived through criticism and survived it. If I take a risk and talk, there is a good chance I will feel better than if I do not.

2. What issues are important to me? Everyone comes to conclusions and has a right to comment on his thoughts. I have a right to have clear opinions. I have a right to say what I think as long as I find a sensitive way to say it. As a matter of fact, it is

each person's obligation in relationships to say what needs to be said.

3. I feel frightened, but I know I must act. When I see that I can speak up for myself (whether or not any one listens to me) then I will not feel so scared. The more I get myself to do this, the better I will get at it.

4. I have strong feelings, so do other people. I can think of a way to express my feelings even though they are strong. It is ok to tell someone I am angry with him or her as long as I do not treat them in an angry or hurtful way.

The Depressed Communicator

Depression is the most common mental health problem in the western world; it is a feeling of hopelessness, helplessness, and despair. Approximately ten percent of men and twenty percent of women in the United States struggle with depression.

Some people experience life as continually discouraging and defeating. Sometimes we feel so bad that we are not able to help ourselves or our children. We may develop a negative and rigid view of our own abilities, other people, and life events. Since we develop a negative view of ourself, we become more pessimistic about our future.

Children of depressed parents are exposed to a range of strong feelings like sadness and despair. The language they hear may be tinged with some hopelessness and defeat. Depressed mothers of infants and children talk less to their children. Researchers compared depressed mothers and nondepressed mothers of two-year-old children.

They interviewed mother-child pairs, observed the mother and child at home numerous times and performed developmental assessments on the children. The results of the study were clear: depressed mothers talked less to their two year olds and inter-acted with them less often than nondepressed mothers. Conse-quently, the children of depressed mothers showed delayed ex-pressive language as well as emotional and behavioral problems.

If depression is a feeling of hopelessness, then communication from depressed parents is going to involve themes of failure and distrust. The child will have to work harder to develop a positive view of himself and his abilities.

Moderate Thoughts To Help Depressed Communication

1. I may do poorly at certain tasks but I do some things quite well. If I appraise myself honestly I could think of many areas where I am adequate or better.

2. I do not know how each task I try will work out until I try. And what if I perform the task at 50 percent, or 75 percent correct, that is better than zero. It is more helpful to think in terms of percentages rather than "all or nothing." I do not want to be a member of the 100 percent club; I am not trying to be perfect, just human.

3. There is no human being on earth that is worthless. We value each human life. We acknowledge each person's potential.

4. Does my worth equal what I can do? A baby is limited in what he can do. Is he useless or worthless? No, my usefulness involves my own personal growth and my ability to use life events as opportunities to grow.

Conclusion

Families can promote healthy communication in children. In the home, the child can learn to develop his individual potential. He can learn to express love and caring and listen to other people. He can learn to think and talk in a way that will allow him to transcend the limitations of troubled communication.

Baha'u'llah *Gleanings from the Writings of Baha'u'llah*, 264, 1976.

Baha'u'llah *Tablets of Baha'u'llah*, p 172-173, 1988.

Cox, A.D., Puckering, C., Pound, A. and Mills, M. *The Impact of Maternal Depression in Young Children.* Journal of Child Psychology and Psychiatry and Allied Disciplines, 1987, vol 28(6), 917-928.

Chapter 9

Angry Talk

"One word may be likened unto fire, and another unto light"

-Baha'u'llah

The angry communicator faces the most difficult challenge in parenting. Angry talk, whether it is consistent or intermittent, harms children.

Researchers have found that one-third of parents do this consistently and another third verbally abuse intermittently. Parents in the remaining third speak harshly with their children infrequently and they are able to recognize it is not healthy.

The angry communicator is often impatient, critical, and abrupt. He does not understand the effect he has on people, particularly on children. If asked how he thinks his behavior affects children, he will diminish the hurtful effect and justify why he speaks too harshly. Thus, the situation usually begins with a perceptual problem on the part of the angry parent in that he does not see the destructiveness of his anger. And there is usually a rationalization for the anger, such as the child deserved it. There is no doubt that people make us angry and that children can be irritating, but this does not justify abusive language. Verbal aggression is as damaging, or more damaging, than physical punishment because it diminishes the child's self-esteem and corrodes the parent-child relationship. Children develop defenses to cope with angry talk; they learn the same angry language and they become unable to talk in a calm, sensitive, and genuine way about their thoughts and feelings.

The results of a recent study highlight the fact that more than two-thirds of all parents use verbal aggression in dealing with their children at one time or another. Verbal abuse includes screaming, yelling, swearing, strong, negative criticism, and harsh unjustified accusations. The researchers proposed that the more verbal aggression experienced by children the higher the rate of childhood psychological and social problems. The evidence supported the idea that the more verbal abuse used by the parent, the greater the likelihood that the child will be physically aggressive, experience school failure, and have interpersonal problems. This finding applies to children of all ages and for both boys and girls. The authors explain their results in the following way:

"We believe that there is a reciprocal relationship between verbal/symbolic aggression by parents and children's behavior problems. Research ...(has) found an escalating feedback loop which can be triggered by either the deviant behavior of the child or by verbally aggressive behavior of the parent. Suppose the situation is one in which the process is triggered by the misbehavior of the child and that the parent responds by verbal aggression such as swearing at the child. This can result in sufficient anger, resentment, and damage to self-esteem that the child engages in additional anti-social behavior. The parents may then intensify their verbal assaults on the child. Thus, the effect of using verbal aggression as a control tactic may be to exacerbate rather than extinguish the problematic behavior" (Vissing and Straus, 1989).

Some families breed anger. Family anger and the tendency to be abusive are transmitted across generations. There is some evidence to show that angry families produce angry children who tend to raise more angry children of their own. From this we can conclude that anger is a learned pattern of dealing with people that is passed on in families. Gary Emery, a psychologist, has written, "...Family violence is transmitted through the generations. That is, children who are abused, neglected, or witnesses to violence in their family of origin are thought to be at an increased risk for continuing the violence in their families of procreation."

Although this intergenerational view of family abuse has been verified in numerous psychological studies, there are exceptions. A notable minority of children reared by angry parents break the cycle of hostility and live a more balanced life style. Estimates show that approximately 30 to 40 percent of abused children grow up to reject family anger for a more peaceful, less reactive approach to life.

Tina remembers the following scene from when she was eight-years-old. She and her sisters had gotten some finger-sized dolls called pinky dolls from the five and dime store in the neighborhood. Making clothes for their dolls was exciting.

Father: What are you doing in here? What are you girls
            doing?
Tina: We're playing with these dolls. We made clothes
            for them out of scraps of fabric.
Father: That's ridiculous. Those dolls are too small. It's
            bad for your eyes to play with dolls that small.
Tina: But we love these dolls...
Father: Shut up! What do you know? Don't you ever talk
            back to me like that? Put these away (sweeps the
            doll scene off the bed and onto the floor with one
            blow) and don't ever let me see them again.
Tina: (crying) But we like them so much. We bought them
            with our own money.
Father: Are you talking back to me? How dare you talk
            back to me! I'm going to give you something to cry

Tina: about. (hits the children) You are all stupid girls!
I wasn't trying to talk back, I just wanted to keep
my dolls and the clothes we made.

Father: You nasty brat. Don't you open your mouth again!
(grabs her and shoves her up against the wall) Do
you hear me?

Abusive parents are ordinary people who have been raised in angry families and who deal ineffectively with stress and problems. Situational factors like financial problems, marital discord, and household chores cause stress and make an angry person likely to be abusive. Abusive parents are triggered by their limited child rearing knowledge, low tolerance for children's crying and fighting, and misunderstanding of children's motivation for misbehavior. Below are some examples of each.

Limited understanding of child development leads some parents to lose their patience with children inappropriately.

Doug lost his patience with his two-year-old son. Doug was taking care of his children one day. He went into the bedroom where his sons were playing, set out clothes for both boys, and told them to get dressed. When he came back ten minutes later, he found that the boys did not obey him. He yelled at the boys for not getting dressed. He did not realize that his two-year-old boy could not dress himself and the four-year-old was in the process of learning this skill.

Squabbling and disputes among children are a normal part of growing up. When we understand child development, we have an idea of when and how to start teaching children to use words and not fists. We train them patiently and help them settle their fights by talking and problem solving. Lena was a mother of four rough and tumble boys. The boys were always rolling around together and wrestling which would, at times, lead to a fistfight. Lena felt angry and irritable and would scream at the boys instead of help them solve their problems by talking. She did not understand that disputes were part of growing up and that her job as parent was to help the boys process what was happening between them. She needed to help her children solve their problems by talking, which would help the boys learn from the conflict.

Tolerance for children's crying and conflict is an important parental skill. When I was twenty-two years old, unmarried and unfamiliar with children, I took a trip with a friend from graduate school and her three young children. I was numb by the time we arrived at our destination; the noise, the squabbling, the fidgeting, and the neediness of the children were all normal and new to me. It takes time to adjust to the level of commotion that children bring to life. One crucial aspect of parenting is the ability to remain calm. This ability requires much motivation, thinking, feeling and talking. Motivation to understand and value human feelings is at the core of patience; it is empathy for what the child is feeling. The adult's internal dialogue goes like this, "This youngster has feelings and sensitivities just like everybody else, she does not know what to do with them, and she needs to express them. She will feel good and learn if I talk to her about her experience, help her understand it, and choose a positive course of action."

The last issue that causes angry talk in families is misunderstanding of children's motivation.

One mother said to her daughter, "You won't eat your broccoli because you are spiteful."

The daughter innocently replied, "No, Mom, I just don't like the taste of broccoli."

Some people just do not like broccoli and there is a way to negotiate with children to get them to eat some vegetables without forcing them to eat what is distasteful to them. We can work out vegetable choices and other problems without attributing ulterior motivations to their actions.

Tina's father continually misunderstood her motivation. Tina remembers standing at the top of a flight of steps, as a seven-year-old, while a few other children were trying to get in the door. Tina did not see the children trying to get in. Her father opened the door and misinterpreted Tina's behavior; he thought she was purposefully trying to keep the children outside. He was furious and did not have the skills or patience to discuss the problem with Tina. Instead, he reflexively yelled at her and kicked her squarely in the back such that she went tumbling down the flight of cement steps. Tina was bruised but she was also humiliated by the assault, which took place in front of the other children.

When the children were all in the house, Tina's father slammed the door leaving her outside at the bottom of the steps.

When parents misinterpret a child's behavior it can lead to harsh and abusive treatment which causes the child to feel confused and angry. After all, from Tina's perspective, she was not doing anything wrong by standing in the doorway and, thus, it felt to her as though her father punished her out of the blue. In this way, anger and angry talk can be passed on down through the generations.

In some families there is intermittent anger from one or both parents. The anger rages violently at times with subsequent periods of calm. The calm can be tense because no one, parents or children, knows when the next episode will come. If the periods of calm are long enough, the children may be lulled into the hope that the anger has gone away.

Yet, this pattern of intermittent anger does not go away and family members live with the possibility of outbursts at any time. When a parent abuses intermittently, a child may come to believe that if only he could try harder, then maybe he could ward off the abuse. Thus, she tries to be perfect: she tries to do and say what is right. She tries to anticipate other people's needs. The abuse comes anyway. She may feel helpless, frightened, and ultimately hopeless as a result. It is easy to see how a child living with this level of fear adopts the "don't feel" and "don't talk" rules that have been previously described. It is simply not safe to feel and talk spontaneously like other children. In the intermittently abusive family another rule is taught, "don't trust." How can you trust people whom you must depend on for your food, shelter, and love when they can turn on you at any time? The child cannot understand there is no clear relationship between her behavior and the parent's tirade; the parent becomes angry because of his or her own problems.

This describes Tina's dilemma. She tried hard to please her parents and at times would meet with their approval. Yet, more often she would be criticized and punished. There was no way for her to know how to be safe and avoid her parents' anger, which made her feel anxious, and on edge. It was not safe to feel her own feelings or speak her own thoughts. Instead, she had to anticipate what to say and do that would keep her safe. When Tina was a child, she would feel anxious and queasy at the sound of her father's car pulling into the driveway. She knew that it often meant trouble.

Tina: I heard Dad's car pull in.

Jerry: Maybe we better turn the TV off.

Tina: Yeah and clean up the ....

Father: What are you doing? You are both lazy and good-for-nothing. Get up there and do something for a change. You are nothing, you are both no good…

Children know angry talk when they hear it. I asked a group of four- and five-year-old children to distinguish angry talk that they wanted to hear from an adult versus talk that they did not want to hear. Each child got a list of choices such as, "I want you to show me good talking from now on.," as opposed to, "You are a brat to talk to me that way." The majority of the children were able to choose the positive language immediately. I also asked the children to think of positive language in situations where they might have heard angry talk. For instance, the children were asked, "What would you say if your mother accidentally spilled milk on the table?" Most of the children found these types of questions humorous and they suggested positive replies: "Try not to spill

•

your milk again." Or "Now you have to clean it up!"

One evening I was feeling particularly tired and I told my two boys to get into bed after reading them a bedtime story. The boys did not obey; they rolled around on the floor, quarreled with each other, and started to pull some books off the shelf. I was getting mad as I tried to calm the baby who wanted to be fed. Then the boys ran into the bathroom for a drink of water, spilled water all over the floor, and slipped in it. They pushed each other around in the water. I tried to be calm but my patience was gone; I called them, they did not listen and that was the last straw. I scolded them brusquely and put them to bed.

As soon as I could, I got to my notebook to try to rethink the situation. My thoughts were racing and they went something like this:

Angry Thoughts

1. I will never get these kids in bed. They are going to evade me all night.

2. They never listen to me and maybe they are undisciplined and unruly children.

3. I am exhausted and I feel like I am going to run out of energy any minute. I am going to collapse or explode.

Angry Feelings

1. (Bad Feelings) I feel desperate, frustrated, and ineffective. I do not feel like a good mother.

2. (Bad/Scared Feelings) I feel like I am getting nowhere with them, I am exasperated.

3. (Bad/Hurt Feelings) I feel tired, angry, upset, worried and all alone.

Rethinking To Be More Moderate

1. I put my kids to bed every night, and every night they resist me in silly ways. It is understandable they do not want to leave me or their fun games. And for some reason kids deplore the thought of dropping off to sleep peacefully; they prefer to fight it. If I am patient and present clear limits, they will do what I ask,

albeit slowly, and we will have a pleasant parting.

2. They do not listen to me some of the time, but they do listen to me most of the time. I would say they listen and obey about 75 percent of the time. I do not want any of us to hold membership in the 100 percent club anyway.

3. I am exhausted. Maybe I will rest on this chair, hold the baby and think up some limit to set as an incentive for the boys. I will tell the boys that I am not going to make waffles in the morning with any boy who is not in his bed by the count of five.

By now you know that by reworking my thoughts along these lines, I am not only going to change my feelings but I am going to talk differently.

Children who are the objects of routine parental anger manifest a variety of problems. There is an interaction between the child's temperament and verbal abuse. In other words, children react differently to verbal abuse based on their nature. A shy, reticent child will feel and behave differently from an outgoing child. Inevitably, however, verbal abuse wounds all children in some way.

Verbally abused children become verbally and physically aggressive. If harsh words are heard at home, then the child will use them both at home and out in the world. Children who are spoken to with anger will have problems with peers. They will be unable to work out amicable friendships with classmates and friends.

Jed was a bully. He had been verbally abused at home by both parents and his reaction to the mean talk was to act out his anger. He was sent to the principal's office often for behavior problems during his fourth- and fifth-grade years. Jed had trouble with schoolwork although he was bright, but his one joy in life was playing football. He was very good at it and was a valuable member of the team. One problem got in his way. He did not get along with his teammates; he criticized them, bullied them, and projected a negative attitude toward them. He treated people in the same way that he had been treated at home.

Impaired social understanding is a common result of too much family anger. Harsh words confuse children. They cannot accurately assess peers' motives when they have known a preponderance of hurt. Their tendency in understanding people is to think negatively and judge harshly. There is a lack of empathy and compassion for other people and their feelings. It is as though the child becomes hardened and has a limited range of feeling for other people.

Depression is another problem that can arise for children who are verbally abused. The child may lack energy and feel sad. He may withdraw and lose interest in the world. A feeling of despondency may emerge where the child feels that anything he says or does may be punished.

Another reaction to verbal abuse is the inability to pay attention and concentrate. Children who cannot focus their attention on learning have trouble in school. The inability to pay attention mixed with depressed feelings and lack of self-efficacy leads to learning problems. Academic failure is frequently associated with children who are mistreated.

Tina remembers the way her father spoke to her. As a young child, her father called her names and made her feel bad and ashamed. As she got older he tried to scare her into behaving the way he wanted her to.

Tina: (at age 12) I like to have long bangs because all the kids in school have long hair. That's the style.

Father: That looks awful. Noooo. You are going to get your bangs cut.

Tina: But I like them this way. I feel better with them a bit longer.

Father: What do you know? Stupid girls. Let me tell you the way it is. I know what teachers like. You are not going to school looking like a jerk.

Tina: Lots of kids have much longer bangs.

96

Father:	You look stupid. All your teachers will know how stupid you are. Get that hair out of your eyes. Ridiculous, ungrateful, lousy brats.
Tina:	But...please don't cut them.
Father:	Where the hell do you think you're going to sleep to night?

Tina was plagued by feelings of being stupid and unacceptable but the idea that she was not going to have a place to sleep that night was terrifying. Her father used threats that undermined her ability to feel safe and protected from the outside world. Verbal abuse is destructive because words that are spoken in frustration by parents are often taken literally by children. That is why they cannot develop healthy peer relationships, perform in school, and become depressed.

Baha'u'llah, *Tablets of Baha'u'llah,* p 172-173, 1988

Emery, Gary E. *Family Violence.* American Psychologist, 1989, 44,2, 321-328.

Garbarino, J., Guttmann, E. and Seeley, J.W. *The Psychologically Battered Child.* Josey-Bass, Inc., San Francisco, 1986,

Vissing, Y.M. and Straus, M. *Verbal Aggression by Parents and Psycho-social Problems of Children.* Family Research Laboratory, University of New Hampshire, 1989.

Chapter 10

Guide Me and Discipline Me, Mom and Dad

"When children have been well loved by their parents, this engenders a responding love in them that makes them want to become grown-ups like their parents and -most of the time- makes them want to please their parents."
                                                            -Benjamin Spock

One of the most difficult aspects of the parent-child relationship is the constancy of care that infants and young children require. Infants and young children need the attentive presence of a parent or caregiver during all of their waking hours. This is no small requirement, as children are awake more than they are asleep. The stress of parenting and the sometimes-annoying behavior of helpless young children makes a heavy burden.

Families may experience discord and marriages may fall apart during the years when children are young and dependent. Most divorces occur for couples between 25 and 38, and this is coincident with the rearing of young children. It is not a coincidence that marriages break up during these child-rearing years. The stress of young children takes its toll.

"The statistics on when people get divorced are chilling: the highest divorce rates are for women at age 30 and men at age 33. As you can see, this means that many people are splitting up with very small children-and perhaps as a result of the unreasonable expectations they may have had." (Hotchner, 1988, p 44)

During their waking hours children alternate between actively exploring their world and trying to get attention from their parents. As children grow, they are capable of amusing themselves for longer periods of time and spending more time in cooperative play with peers. This process occurs slowly over the period of five years. Children vary a great deal in terms of their capacity to play independently and with peers. The young child needs protection from physical harm, nurturing, intellectual stimulation, and guidance.

Parents are busy people. They have many other household duties to perform while they are taking care of their children, not to mention jobs they may have outside the home. In caring for children and a home, it may feel that there is more work to do than hours to do it.

Parents are not entertainers. Children would not learn how to play independently if their parent amused them all the time. Although parents are not entertainers, they are educators and guides. As children play during the day, they require assistance from their parents as they learn about peer relationships, independence, and self control.

Parents determine how the home will function on two levels: 1) general structure of the day, and 2) interpersonal interactions. The general structure of the day involves where the children play, how much exercise they get, how much reading and sharing of books goes on, what foods they eat and when, how the television is used, what friends come to the home, and many other organizational features. Moms and Dads who are interested and available can structure the home and orchestrate a healthy and industrious environment. Parents structure a child's day by choosing certain day care centers, camps, after-school programs, or home-care situations which conform to their expectations of quality.

The second level of availability for a parent is the ability to help with interpersonal relationships. Parents are available for the routine questions, comments, and disputes. "Mommy he made fun of my hair." "I don't want to finish my carrots." "She wrecked up my fort again." "How do you spell supercalifragilistic?" "I can't open the door." "Have you seen my baseball cap?" "She told me to shut-up." "I want to feed the cat."

The mother is the first educator of the child. The family environment, from birth until seven years old, is the most critical for the child. During the first seven years of life, a child's character and identity are formed. After this time, it is difficult to modify his personality. Guidance, availability, and discipline are critical during this early seven-year period. The child typically spends more time with his mother than with any other human being until she attends school. Mothers educate their children in the lessons of life including emotional, social, spiritual, physical, linguistic, and intellectual. In order for the child to emerge from these years as a confident, compassionate and capable human being, a great deal of talking takes place.

In 1931 a child guidance manual was written by Ray C. Berry and published by the National Child Research Clinic. In this manual parents were warned against talking to children about their thoughts and feelings since this would encourage them to be "self-conscious."

"Self-consciousness is a result of thinking too much about oneself. In order to help a child overcome this attitude of mind, talk to him about other children and little about himself. Make it the rule to introduce the thought, of other children into his mind often. For example, instead of saying, 'Don't you think this is delicious ice cream?' say, 'Don't you wish Johnnie (or James or some other playmate) could enjoy this ice cream with us?'...Instead of asking your son, 'How do you like this cake?' say, 'Don't you think grandmother would like this cake - it is her favorite flavor."

Needless to say, times have changed. We help our children to become comfortable with their thoughts and feelings. To the extent that we guide our child by talking to him about himself, his thoughts, his emotions and his speech, he will grow to understand and value himself. To the extent that we listen to our child, he will listen to his own thoughts and feelings and develop self-confidence and self-reliance. To the extent that we honor our child's choices and decisions, he can learn to trust. This guiding process helps children to develop a solid sense of themselves, which is the basis for altruism and social action.

The idea of guidance and support in raising children is difficult to grasp if one's own childhood was difficult. Tina wondered why her mother made the child rearing decisions that she did. Tina's mother chose to stay married to Tina's father who was clearly abusive to her and her children. Tina's mother talked a great deal about her own suffering with her young daughters, yet she was helpless to improve her life. As Tina learned more about her mother's childhood, this inability to change became more understandable, but still not acceptable. Tina's mother did not have a father at home; he left her mother (Tina's grandmother) when she was two, and she never saw him again. Tina's mother was bounced back and forth between her mother and her grandmother, lived in poverty, and spent an inordinate amount of time alone. Tina's mother described the summer she spent when she was eight or nine years old.

"My own mother worked in a factory six days a week on twelve hour shifts. I stayed alone in a two-room apartment waiting for my exhausted mother to return at seven o'clock in the evening. All my mother could do was go to sleep leaving me alone once again. I remember my mother taking me with her from my grandmother's house for the summer because she said she did not want to be alone. But I was alone and this went on day after day for the whole summer. There was no TV, no one to talk to, and nowhere to go. Sometimes I would go down to the sidewalk outside our apartment building and look at the people go by. Then I would go back up to the apartment and draw. I think drawing pictures was the way I survived that summer."

Tina's mother had five children over the course of six years and continued to work outside the home during this period of time. Within a few years Tina's mother went back to college to work for a degree. Tina's father also worked during the day and went to school at night. Anyone familiar with family life can calculate the amount of time and caring that might have been left over for five children after Tina's parents worked, attended classes, did school work, and performed their household chores.

Adult:	Tina, what was it like for you growing up? How can you describe what it felt like to be a child?
Tina:	I felt unimportant and like I was a burden. No one showed any interest my life. No one talked to me.
Adult:	Did you ever feel like an adult was happy to see you?
Tina:	Never. I felt like I was a problem, always in the way and always needing too much.
Adult:	How did you cope with these feelings?
Tina:	I realized that the only way my parents would ever notice me was if I cleaned, cooked, did laundry or took care of the younger ones. When I realized this, I tried as hard as I could to work and do chores to please my parents.
Adult:	So you began to learn that you were not important as a person, but the work that you did would get you some reward. In other words, your value as a person became linked with your ability to work.
Tina:	Yes, I tried hard to please my parents by being as good as I could be and working as hard as I could.

Adult:	How did this fit in with your father's anger?
Tina:	I feared my father's anger so much. It could come at any time. So I worked and tried to please my parents in order to avoid my father's temper.
Adult:	Who did you go to when you were hurt and confused?
Tina:	I tried not to have those feelings because that was a sign of weakness according to my parents. I could never show my feelings or I would be either punished or ridiculed.
Adult:	So who was there for you when you were young and needed help talking and working out feelings?
Tina:	No one.

Children do not grow up to be emotionally healthy without communication. Neglect sows the seeds for the internal rules that abused children learn: Don't Feel and Don't Trust. Tina lived in fear of her father. She grew up in a home without an adult who was present and caring. Her way of coping with the abuse and the neglect was to try as hard as she could to do the household chores and please her parents. The irony is that she could never please them, not because she was not pleasing but because it was impossible to please them.

Tina survived psychologically by telling herself that love was possible. She told herself, "Work harder and be more perfect." If she could just keep trying, then she would finally please her parents and get them to stop fighting and show love. It was more acceptable to Tina to believe she was unlovable, unworthy and defective, than to believe there was something seriously wrong with her family.

Guidance requires talking and listening. An infant knows nothing of table manners yet a seven-year-old, if properly trained, can eat politely in an elegant dining room. An infant possesses the rudiments for vocal exchange with people; a ten-year-old, raised in a rich language environment, can wax poetic. An infant knows nothing of morals and values; a fourteen-year-old can listen for her own inner voice and speak out for social change.

Kent was five years old and had been thrown out of four preschool programs. His mother, Barb, was 20 years old, unmarried, on welfare, and had no family or friends. She had never seen Kent's father again after she found out she was pregnant. Barb looked masculine and talked as if driven by a motor. She believed that people hated her.

Barb could not tolerate being touched. She said, "I got banged up when I was drunk and stoned." Barb is becoming more aware of why she cannot be touched. She has related some scattered memories of sexual and physical abuse but is struggling to understand how this renders her incapable of trusting people's physical or emotional contact.

Kent is an active, vibrant child. He does not give up. The first time I met Barb and Kent, he went up to his mother after about fifteen minutes in my office. First he sat close to her and waited. Then he leaned over to her and nudged her with his shoulder. She pushed him away. He put his foot on her knee. She lifted his foot and shoved it hard. Kent fell back against a table. His mother did not stop talking during this time.

Kent sat on the floor hurting. I waited for Barb to go to him but she did not. I went to him and asked if he was all right. He looked at me and nodded grimly. I sat on the floor next to Kent as Barb babbled on. We took some toys out of a box. Kent showed me the toys he liked and eventually he put a toy on my knee. He looked at me cautiously. He put another toy in my hand and touched my hand. I put a toy in his hand and touched his hand.

Barb feels rage and terror beyond what she can tolerate when she is touched. Her emotions range from irritation to fury even when she is not being touched. She did not give Kent up for adoption when he was born because she felt some loving feelings for him. Those feelings are foreign to her and she does not have them now. She feels overwhelmed and totally incapable of parenting Kent.

Barb and Kent come to see me every week. They now go to see a nurse practitioner every week and they go to see the school psychologist every week. The three helpers consult to figure out how to help Barb and Kent.

Me: Barb, how do you feel about seeing me, the nurse, and the school psychologist?

Barb: It's ok. I know every week I can tell each of you what happened with Kent. He is so bad I can't stand it.

Me: Why do you think we are all interested in you and Kent?

Barb: I don't know. It just seems like you guys just can understand what I'm going through with this brat. He's trouble and he makes my life miserable. Why did I get stuck with such a monster? You know what he did....

Me: Kent can be tough at times but you are sticking with him. And you have three people who want to stick with you. How come?

Barb: You have to. Kent has tantrums all the time just to piss me off. Ask your secretary what he did before you came in. He is a snake. He is so mean and sneaky. There is no controlling him. I just wish I could get rid of him...

Me: Barb, you have not gotten rid of him and he has made your life harder. You feed him, you bathe him, and you put clean clothes on him everyday. This is a good start. You also take him to see me, the nurse, and the school psychologist. Why?

Barb: Because he is a wreck and so am I. I just don't know why he can't sit and watch TV. No, he has to jump around...

Me: Barb, back to my question. How come we stick with you? You know we do not have to. I look forward to seeing you and Kent.

Barb: I don't know why. He is a rotten kid. He ran away from me yesterday...

Me:	Do you believe I look forward to seeing you?
Barb:	No. Sometimes. No. Sometimes. Well, but we drive you crazy. You know he pulled all the magazines off the shelf...
Me:	You do drive me crazy at times and you probably drive the Nurse, Clair, and Dr. Chuck crazy too. But why do we all keep getting together with you? Come on, answer me!
Barb:	You think I'm ok. But Kent threw all his toys...
Me:	Barb, you got it. I do like you and I care about what happens to you and Kent.
Barb:	So do Nurse Clair and Dr. Chuck. Kent takes apart their office...
Me:	Barb, we don't care if Kent does stuff in our offices. We want you to know we care.
Barb:	And you care about Kent.
Me:	And we care about how you take care of Kent.

It is not easy to keep Barb on the topic but a magnificent change has taken place. She does not say that no one cares about her and Kent any more. This caring has translated into Barb's trying harder to guide Kent. She still cannot touch Kent but she can praise him three times during each session. Barb reports to me what Kent did well during the week before she tells me how bad he was. And Barb is considering making friends with a neighbor.

Discipline is not a separate parental activity to be distinguished from routine interactions. An integral part of guidance is correction. The motivation-thinking-feeling-talking model helps us to understand how discipline works in the context of availability. Micca is motivated to be a good girl and she wants to do the right thing, but she slips. Micca thinks, "Mom is not looking and now is my chance to snatch a cookie."

When Mom talks to Micca about stealing the cookie, she asks if Micca took the cookie. If Micca says, "Yes," then Mom praises her for telling the truth. If Micca says, "No," then Mom gently encourages Micca to tell the truth and then praises her for telling the truth. Simple descriptive praise is best. "I am happy that you told me the truth about the cookie."

After the praise, Mom could use logical consequences as a form of discipline if she feels more is needed.

"I am disappointed in you and I will not be able to give you this cookie for dessert tonight."

With our language we guide children and help them to see their mistakes. We talk to them about the feelings and thoughts behind the mistakes. We reflect their words and behavior back to them so they can understand the impact they made. At times we even have to use words to remove them from social activity when they have made mistakes. We call this time when children have to leave the social interactions a "time out" session. I recommend time out for young children starting at about 3 years and going on to the age of about nine or ten. If time out is used with sensitivity, consistency, and clarity early in a child's life, it is not necessary to use it beyond age ten. At that time, verbal means including reasoning, expressing disapproval, and withdrawing rewards take precedence.

In using time out, when the child is willing to cooperate, he can come back to the ongoing activity. Time out literally means a time out from the possibility of rewards. So, when a child is sent to time out for a mistake, he is removed from the chance to have fun and/or be in the company of other people.

Lynn Clark, Ph.D., a behavioral psychologist, wrote a book for parents explaining how to use time out effectively. He has done a wonderful job describing how and when to use time out and how to trouble shoot problems that arise while using time out.

To use time out effectively, parents must be able to communicate with their children. Before parents begin, they discuss time-out with one another and make decisions about how, when, and where to use it. The next step involves talking to the child about time out and explaining to him what it is, when it will be used, and how it works. Time out should not take place in a child's bedroom or playroom. Time out works best if the child is sent to a quiet, out-of-the-way place like the hallway or laundry area (or Outer Mongolia). He stands in time out for the number of minutes that corresponds to his age: for instance three year olds get three minutes, ten year olds get ten minutes. The child stays in time out until she hears the timer ring. Parents set a timer to help themselves and the child remain clear about how long they have to stand in time out.

Use time out as a last resort and do not use it more than twice a day. When your child behaves in a way you do not approve, tell him it is time for a time out. State what she did wrong in the same sentence such as "You have to have a time out now because you hit your brother." Make sure your child can hear the timer when it rings. Wait for the timer without looking at your child or giving her any attention.

Steps For Time Out
1. Parents discuss time out and how to use it.
2. Parents talk with children about time out, why they are going to use it, and how they will use it.
3. When an undesirable behavior occurs, parents state that child will have a time out and what went wrong in one sentence.
4. Parents place the timer within earshot of child and set it for the number of minutes that corresponds to the child's age.
5. Parents wait for the timer to go off without interacting with the child at all.
6. Parents strictly avoid lecturing, criticizing, blaming, or embarrassing the child. Time out is not done in front of other people.

Here is an example of a time out done well by both parent and youngster. Todd and Tyler are brothers and they are five years old and seven years old respectively. They like to play together but lately Tyler has been too rough with Todd. Both boys are playing on their swing set and Tyler pushes Todd off the monkey bars. Mom and Dad are working around the yard and they see this problem unfold. Dad comforts Todd while Mom calmly calls out to Tyler, "I am angry with you because you have been told not to push your brother that way and now you have to go into time out." Mom and Tyler go into the house, Tyler stands in the hallway time out spot, and Mom puts the timer on for seven minutes. Mom pretends to be busy in the kitchen while she waits and she does not let Tyler see her glance into the hallway for a peek at him.

Three five-year-old boys were playing in the yard, while their fathers were sitting on a nearby porch. The fathers could not see the boys in all parts of the yard. The boys found sticks that had nails on them and started to fight and threaten each other. The fathers yelled to their sons to put the sticks down. The third boy continued to swing his stick dangerously. The third boy's father had to run through the house, around the back yard and through the side yard to get to his son and hold his arms to make him stop.

Some danger threatened all three boys and their fathers knew it. The first two boys knew their fathers were serious when they said put the sticks down. The first boy was afraid of his father and knew that an angry tone of voice resulted in harsh punishment. The boy knew he could expect angry talk or physical punishment if he did not obey. This boy was not able to talk to his father about the dispute; his father did not want to talk about it nor did he value communication. Control and power are the issues at hand.

The second boy learned that a certain tone of voice and expression of urgency from his father signaled it was time to listen. He knew that some verbal commands from his parents were negotiable and some were not. Yet, this child knew that he could talk to his parents about his feelings when the time was right and he felt free to discuss issues with them.

The second boy's parents had been teaching the motivation-thinking-feeling talking process to him as he grew up. This came in handy when they had their talks. The second boy's thoughts went something like this when he opened the conversation with his parents later on.

Thoughts About The Fight
1. "What's the big deal? We can handle sticks with nails on them. We are all in second grade now."
2. "My parents get too upset, those sticks were not dangerous because we were just swinging them and we did not intend to him each other."
3. "My parents do not trust me."

Feelings About The Fight
1. Hurt Feelings. "I am so frustrated that they treat me like a baby."
2. Sad Feelings. "I feel misunderstood and upset."
3. Angry Feelings. "I am so angry that they do not trust me."

Reworking The Thoughts
1. "Our intentions are good, we would not hit each other on purpose but there might be an accident. If a boy got cut with an old rusty nail, he might have to go to the hospital for a shot. Maybe Mom and Dad just want to prevent this."
2. "My parents believe our intent is to be good; they worry about accidents."
3. "My parents may overprotect me sometimes, but they do trust me to do some risky things when they feel I can handle it."
The third boy's parents have not taught him to listen to them. The boy knows there is no meaningful consequence for his behavior. The parents apply some punishment they believe should be effective but it is not. When parents do not insist that their words are important and must be respected, then children fail to learn the power of words.

The first boy has been treated too harshly by his parents and he is afraid of them. When parents are too harsh, rigid, and punitive we call their parenting style authoritarian. Authoritarian parents go overboard with control and restraint such that they hurt and abuse their children. Their children's thinking, feeling, talking, and behavior is not as important as the parent's ego and need for power. This type of parenting can be described as the "cement slab approach." The parent is as immovable and unapproachable as a cement slab. You cannot reason with a cement slab and their is no empathy or flexibility. A child, such as the first boy, would be hurt, angry and frustrated in trying to work with his "cement slab" parent.

Some parents who use the cement slab approach believe that hitting, spanking, and slapping children is acceptable. Children's Hospital at Dartmouth, NH, has listed five reasons why we do not spank children:

1. Spanking teaches children they do not have control over their behavior. Lack of this inner control can block children's ability to solve problems and make decisions on their own.

2. Spanking can teach children to rely on others for control of their behavior. Children who learn to rely on external controls are more apt to let circumstances, events, and others influence their actions rather than using their own resources.

3. Spanking is not an effective means of changing behavior. The effects of spanking are immediate but usually are short term.

4. Spanking can teach children to seek revenge or retaliate against the punisher. It teaches children to hate, fear, and/or avoid the punisher. Children don't easily forget the pain and humiliation of hitting.

5. Spanking tells a child what not to do. It does not teach them appropriate behavior; it teaches them that hitting is OK.

The second boy listens to his father because he reads the urgency in the father's voice and face, but he can be confident that his feelings and reactions will be processed at a later time. This type of parent is referred to as an "authoritative" parent because he has authority but he uses it wisely and justly. He is not an unapproachable cement slab; he is more like a willow tree that bends with the wind. A willow tree rarely breaks in a strong wind because it is flexible, yielding, and strong also. Likewise, the second father is flexible in his approach, willing to entertain alternatives and receptive to feelings. "Willow tree" parents' goal is to problem solve with their children and work toward solutions that work for everyone. These parents seek win-win solutions.

"Mush bowl" parenting is not a particularly flattering term. The third type of parenting is the most disastrous in its negative effects on children. These parents are usually called permissive parents because they permit all sorts of thinking, talking, and behavior that is inappropriate and unhealthy for children. Mush bowl communication has no (or few) boundaries such that children are in control of what happens. There is no give and take in interactions with mush bowl parenting because the children are in control and call the shots. The parents are unwilling or unable to stand their ground and guide the child toward acceptable behavior. This is extremely harmful for children and of the three types of parenting it has the worst result.

The third boy, in the example of the sticks with nails on them, could not obtain and use safety information from his father. There was no trust or basis for belief in what the father had to say to his son. No limits or consequences had been set before this time for the boy to remember. The only recourse for this father was to run through the house to the outside and grab the stick away from his son.

Mush Bowl Talking
Mother: (to her three-year-old child): I don't want you to scratch
　　　　Jenny.

Daughter:I can. (she scratches her playmate Jenny)
Mother: Oh, I don't know what to do with you. (no consequence provided)

Willow Tree Talking

Mother: If you scratch Jenny one more time you will have a time out.
Daughter:I can. (she scratches her playmate Jenny)
Mother: No, I will not allow that and now you will have a time out. (takes her to remote spot in hallway, sets timer for three minutes) Now you will stay here until the timer rings. (mother watches from a far, the timer rings).

Mush Bowl Talking

Father: (to nine-year-old daughter) Please do not light that match for the fireplace while I am out in the garage. Later when I am done with the garbage we will light it together.
Daughter:(lights the match)
Father: (comes in from garage) I smell smoke. What were you doing?
Daughter:Nothing.
Father: But where did this smoke come from?
Daughter:Oh you never believe me.
Father: Well, I don't know what you did.

Willow Tree Talking

Father: (to nine-year-old daughter) Please do not light that match while I am out in the garage. Later when I am done with the garbage we will light it together.
Daughter:(lights the match)
Father: (comes in from garage) I smell smoke. What were you doing?
Daughter:Nothing.

Father: That is not possible. When I left there was no smoke, now there is smoke. Tell me what you did.

Daughter: I tried striking this match to see if it would work.

Father: I asked you to wait for me to do that. It is very dangerous for you to light a fire alone. Now I am going to take the matches away and we will not do that together until tomorrow.

Mush Bowl Talking

Mother: Let's get in the car because it is just about time to go to soccer. (to fourteen year old son)

Son: I can't find my soccer cleat.

Mother: Where do you think it could be?

Son: I could not find it after last week's game. I might have lost it last week.

Mother: This is the second pair of cleats you have lost in one year and they are expensive.

Son: What am I supposed to do about it? Just buy me another pair.

Mother: I guess we will have time to go to the store.

Willow Tree Talking

Mother: Let's get in the car because it is just about time to go to soccer. (to fourteen year old son)

Son: I can't find my soccer cleat.

Mother: Where do you think it could be?

Son: I could not find it after last week's game. I might have lost it last week.

Mother: This is the second pair of cleats you have lost in one year and they are expensive. What is happening?

Son: I don't know.

Mother: I am upset about this. I will not buy you another pair of cleats. You will have to earn the money to buy them and you will have to work out with your soccer coach what will happen to you today given that you have no cleats.

Mush Bowl Talking

Mother: (to her sixteen-year-old daughter) I know, dear, but I just can't help the way your brother talks.

Daughter: I can't stand him and I can't stand you either. You are both idiots. (stomps out of house to go to school then later she calls Mother from school)

Daughter: Mom, I want you to bring my book from off my desk to me at school.

Mother: Well, ok Dear., I will be there soon.

Daughter: Don't take too long.

Willow Tree Talking

Mother: (to her sixteen year old daughter) I know it upsets you when your brother talks that way but I would like you to be able to state your feelings in a clear and civil way.

Daughter: I can't stand him and I can't stand you either. You are both idiots. (stomps out of house to go to school then later she calls Mother from school)

Daughter: Mom, I want you to bring my book from off my desk to me at school.

Mother: First of all, I feel bad about the way you spoke to me this morning. I can not talk about the book until you address what happened this morning.

Daughter: I was mad.

Mother: I know you were mad and it is ok to be mad and to tell us about it but it is not ok to be rude to us.

Daughter: I don't care about you, just bring me my book.

Mother: Not until you can discuss this civilly with me.

Or Another Alternative

Daughter: I do care about your feelings and I am sorry. What do you think about the book?

Mother: I need to talk about this problem further when you get home. If you can promise to talk about it later then I will bring you the book.

Harris Clemes and Reynold Bean are psychologists who explain the importance of setting clear limits.

"Children who grow up in a home that doesn't have clear rules and limits for behavior will experience great anxiety and confusion. If children are anxious and confused, it is difficult for them to exercise the self-discipline required to manage their own behavior. They are more likely to misbehave, and will have problems following directions and fulfilling responsibilities" (p 65).

Baumrind, Diana *Current patterns of parental authority.* Developmental Psychology Monographs, 4 (1, Part 2), 1971.

Berry, Ray C. *Developing Admirable Manners,* National Child Research Clinic, 1931.

Clark, Lynn SOS, *Help for Parents,* Parents Press, Bowling Green, Kentucky, 1985.

Clemes, Harris and Bean, Reynold *How to Teach Children Responsibility,* Enrich/Ohaus, San Jose, CA, 1983.

Hotchner, Tracy *Childbirth and Marriage*, Avon Books, New York, 1988.

Spock, Benjamin *Dr. Spock On Parenting.* Simon and Schuster, New York, 1988.

Chapter 11

Pitfalls in Children's Verbal Performances

"...Wounds will heal over if feelings find full acceptance."

Alice Miller

The verbal performances of children can be dramatic. In a family, one may find a two year old gleefully reporting how liquid soap feels as he sprinkles it on the kitchen floor, while a six year old wails that she is starving, and an eight year old methodically narrates the events of a baseball game. Each child has a need to express himself.

Mom tells Tom he cannot pour soap on the floor but he can use it to help wash some dishes. She allows Molly to have an apple before dinner, and explains to Joe that she is still listening in spite of the interruptions. It is not easy for children to learn how to talk and how to fit their talk into a busy family life. Inevitably there will be mistakes. This chapter focuses on some pitfalls in children's talk, and how parents can pull them out of the quagmire. Notice that teaching children communication skills means paying attention to their feelings as we support them in their efforts to think, feel, and talk.

Words are learned by actively piecing together bits of meaning;

children do not memorize words, and neither do they attach words to physical objects by rote. All two-year-old children understand the meaning of "cup," and can pick out a cup from among other items on a table and say the word in an appropriate context. This kind of creative thinking is used throughout development as children grasp ever more complex ideas. We have all heard youngsters say, "I'm starving to death," when they meant they feel hungry, or, "I'm freezing and I'm going to turn into ice," when they need to put on a sweater. Unfortunately, it is not uncommon to hear a child say, "I hate that," or "I hate you," without understanding the impact of the words.

These expressions "starving, freezing and hate" and many others like them, are pitfalls for children because the words do not accurately express what the child thinks and feels. Feelings are relative, in that most children have never known starvation, exposure to the elements, or even profound loathing. Parents can guide children to use better words as they suggest, "I think you are hungry, but probably not starving." "How about putting on your sweater, because you are chilly, but probably not frozen." Likewise, parents can explain, "I think you feel angry but that strong feeling will fade away in time. Real hate is so strong and deep that is does not fade away"

Consider nine-year-old Paul, who bragged that he did everything earlier and better than his younger brother, Pete. Whenever the younger brother learned a new skill, like riding a two-wheel bike, Paul remembered that he learned it faster and at an earlier age. The boy's parents noticed this tendency but felt sorry for Paul; they did not correct Paul. But what about Pete?

Paul's parents decided to intervene when he began to brag in a way that was false because they realized this hurt both boys. Paul was struggling with worried feelings since he was making himself look better than he actually was, and Pete would feel bad about himself if his accomplishments were consistently put down. There are pitfalls in children's language performances that occur regularly in conversations with parents: name calling, teasing, and game playing with talk

When Cara calls her brother a dodo-head the first time, a reminder from Mom or Dad explaining that name-calling hurts brother's feelings and a time-out is in order. Most children experiment with name-calling and bad words. Children need to understand that their parents do not approve. It hurts other people and it does not solve problems. Parents can explain, "If you are angry or hurt by another child, then say so. Instead of name-calling, tell the other person exactly what he did to hurt you. Be specific. When you feel upset or hurt by another person, there is a legitimate reason for your feelings; let the person know what happened and how it affected you."

Teasing is like name-calling; it is an indirect way to express feelings and it can humiliate people. When Johnny taunts James by saying he can't kick a soccer ball three inches or that Mary will fall flat on her face if she tries to do a cartwheel, that is teasing. Children need to hear from their parents that all people have feelings just as they do. Underneath the words in name-calling and teasing are thoughts and feelings that need to be expressed. Adults can help the teaser find a better way to say what he wants to say, and support the teasee when he tells how he feels about his teasing and name-calling.

If children swear, threaten, and denigrate other people, then there is something wrong in their life and they need some help. To assist a child who is teasing, name-calling and/or swearing, it is necessary to launch a three-part plan. First, open up a dialogue with the child about what he is thinking and feeling. What is going on inside of him? Who is bothering him? What would he like to say to Mom or Dad or Grandpa or sister? Give him the chance to say what is really happening to him. LISTEN TO HIM. Second, explain to him that you want to know what he is thinking and feeling but that it is hard for you to hear teasing, name-calling, or swearing. Third, tell him about your own feelings. Explain to him how you feel when you are angry or hurt. Show him that you feel like lashing out at people, too, sometimes and tell him about a time when you did this. What did you feel afterward? What would you like to do that would work better?

Here is an example of Part One of the three-fold plan to combat teasing and name-calling.

Mother: You have been teasing your friends this afternoon and I heard some bad words a little while ago. What's going on with you today?

Fay: (age 6) Annie keeps pushing me around and they keep playing all the games they want to play. It's not fair because I want them to play some of my games. (cries)

Mother: Could it be that you are angry? or sad?

Fay: Yes, I am very angry because they are just not being fair.

Mother: Yes, it sounds like they are not being fair with you. That would make me angry too. What would you like them to do for you?

Fay: I want to play dress up and they just want to go downstairs and do gymnastics.

Mother: Could you ask them for a compromise? Would you be willing to play gymnastics for a while then play dress up after that?

Fay: Well, I'll ask them. Could we put make-up on?

Mother: OK.

Here is an example of Part Two.

Mother: Boys, here's fair warning. I really do not want to hear any bad words while you are playing video games. (a few minutes later)

Boys: (bad words)

Mother: I gave you all a fair warning and you did not listen to me about the bad language. I am going to turn this game off for ten minutes. (logical consequence method)

Here is an example of part three.

Father: I was very angry with you, Carl, because I did not like the way you were talking to your mother. I did swear at you and now I feel very bad about it.

Carl: (age 9) You were so angry, you looked scary, and you did not even look like yourself.

Father: I did not feel like myself. I had a bad day at work and I did not sleep much the night before. So when I got home and saw you were giving your mother a hard time, I lost my temper. I am sorry.

Carl: Why is it ok for you to lose self-control and swear and make a scene but it is not ok for me?

Father: It is not ok for me, and it is not ok for you. The reason I decided to talk to you about it is so that you would understand why I lost my temper and swore and how bad I feel about it.

Carl: But I get so mad sometimes just like you.

Father: We need to find a better way to work out our anger. I know I have to work on mine and I would like you to work on yours.

A cunning six-year-old boy, Brett, convinced his parents that he was afraid of them. He did not act afraid. Rather, he said he was scared every time they warned him to behave. Brett realized he could worry his parents by claiming to be afraid. His father had started to use time-out and Brett did not like it. Game playing is the next verbal pitfall that families encounter as they navigate their way through family life. Brett did not understand that direct statements about his thoughts and feelings would work better. His parents tended to be permissive (or mush bowl). Thus, Brett felt free to manipulate them.

My own children have said they were hungry when they really wanted me to tend to them, or they said they were tired when they really wanted me to hold them. Our goal as parents is to teach children to speak directly about what they want.

Brett's father asked him if he had homework one evening just as he was about to tune in to an interesting TV show. Brett replied, "No, I do not think so." But later, when his father was looking through Brett's backpack, he found some math work sheets. He took them to Brett and asked, "What are these?" Brett looked nervous, and said that he must have forgotten about his homework. The three-fold plan for teasing and name-calling works here, too.

Father: Brett, I think you pretended not to have homework because you wanted to watch TV. Tell me what you were thinking and feeling about doing your homework?

Brett: I just wanted to watch the TV show.

Father: So you said something that was not true in order to get what you wanted. What is a better way to handle that?

Brett: I don't know.

Father: You can tell me if you felt worried that I would not listen to you about TV. Could it be that you are worried I will not be flexible with you, and try to compromise?

Brett: I am worried that you won't understand how much I want to watch the show.

Father: I want to compromise with you. I want you to be able to watch the show and get your homework done too. How can we do that?

Brett: Ask me about homework as soon as you get home and I'll do it before the show or after it.

Father: I would like you to do it before the show and I would be happy to remind you when I get home. How about that?

Brett: OK.

The second step in the plan would involve a follow through consequence if Brett did not do his homework when his father reminded him about it. The logical consequence of not seeing the show would work. The third step would require the father to think of a time when he tried to wiggle out of some responsibility, and how he felt about it.

Thus far we have looked at pitfalls in children's conversations with adults. There are always two sides to every story. To conclude, I will list some pitfalls in parents' performance with children. We cannot follow each guideline all the time. The following list is like a target. We will not always hit the bull's eye but we can aim in the right direction.

Conversational "Do nots" With Children
1. Do not lecture to children. Say no more than three sentences in a row. When we lecture to them, we imply that we are smarter, stronger, and superior to them. We are their parents and it is our job to train, guide, and teach children. Instead of lecturing to children, start a dialogue with them. Make a statement, then ask them how they feel or what they think.

2. Do not yell at children. If we yell, then they will yell. It is possible to be firm without yelling. Just like with lecturing, children feel degraded when we yell.

3. Do not blame or shame children. Avoid "YOU" statements. Do not point out what the child did wrong. It is far more difficult and far more effective to use an "I" statement. "I" statements reflect how we feel about the talk or behavior that is a problem. For instance, "I am sad when I hear you yell at your brother." "I feel mad when I hear bad words."

4. Do not criticize children. Criticizing a person is like cutting them; it hurts, it is destructive, and it takes lots of time to heal. There are effective and less punitive ways of getting people and children to change. Use "I" statements, describe your feelings

and reactions and let them know how their behavior affects you.

5. Do not mind-read. It is wise not to assume we know what another person is thinking, feeling, or what he is going to say.

It is better to ask him directly.

6. Do not ignore children. Respond with words or gestures. If you cannot talk because you are upset, say that. Everyone needs a cooling off period when they are emotional and it is important to state that you need this when you do.

Conversational Do's With Children

1. Do take short turns in conversations with children and make sure you give them ample time to express themselves. Help them take their turn by asking questions, maintaining eye contact, and listening to what they say. Respond to what the child says and then make your point.

2. Do speak in a natural tone of voice to children. Tell them how you feel in a serious and firm voice, if need be. If you are angry say, "I am angry with this kind of talking." Then provide a consequence for their behavior.

3. Do use "I" statements and explain how you feel about the child's actions or talk. Say, "I am mad at you now" instead of "You make me mad." There is a big difference between these two statements. The first means I take responsibility for my own feelings and the way I express them. When I feel there is something wrong I am going to bring it up and work on the problem. This may result in a productive talk about behavior and consequences.

4. Do explain clearly and firmly thoughts and feelings about the child's behavior using "I" statements. For instance, a mother can explain her feelings when her eight-year-old boy rides his bike too close to the highway. "I was scared when I heard you were up near Route 108. I am worried that you are going to get hit by a car because that is a busy road."

5. Do ask questions to find out what is on a child's mind. Paraphrase what they say to you and check it out: Did I get that

right? Did I get your message? Do you think I understand? Do validate what your child says to you, "You have a good point." "I can understand why you believe that explanation." "I see that you have thought about that a great deal."

6. Do speak whenever your child speaks to you even if you do not like what she is saying. Tell her if you are not able to talk to her. Tell her that you need to cool off before you can talk to her.

Miller, Alice Thou Shalt Not Be Aware. Meridian/Penguin Books, New York, 1986.

Chapter 12

Moving Toward the Teenage Years

"Life is struggle and striving, development and growth...Certainly its positive accomplishments are important, but also the striving itself is of intrinsic value."
-Karen Horney

Adolescents are confusing to us because their bodies look adult long before their thinking and feeling catch up. It is common for us to expect an older child to know more than he can actually understand about his inner life or other people's behavior. As adults, we sometimes take for granted the lessons we have learned gradually through experience. There are a number of particular learning experiences that adults typically understand, but are missing in the way the child from ten to fourteen thinks, feels, and talks.

The thinking-feeling-talking cycle is relevant to adolescent communication because adolescents have the capacity to think, feel, and express themselves like adults. Yet, they have not had as much practice or experience. Adolescents are sometimes not comfortable with the types of responses they get from their parents. It is a difficult feat for parents to express understanding of their child's feelings and, without alienating him, urge him on toward mature thinking. To validate feelings, we acknowledge the child's emotions in an accepting way, strong feelings included. Here are examples of parent's response to the adolescent:

1. "I know you hate what I said and that you are furious with me right now."
2. "I hear you saying you are angry with my behavior."
3. "I see that you are furious that I made plans already."
4. "Could it be that you are both hurt and angry with what just happened?"
5. "I want to know how you feel even if it is hard to hear it."

According to the thinking-feeling-talking model, the reason adolescents have some difficult feelings is that their thinking has not fully developed. If we work to help them understand and modify their thoughts, they begin to feel better. When they feel better, it is easier for them to talk more and participate in a conversation.

Susan and her mother had a harmonious relationship. Yet, when Susan turned fourteen, she wanted more freedom to stop at friends' houses after school.

Susan would start by saying, "You never let me go anywhere."

Susan's mother would become upset and start lecturing Susan in this way, "I try to do so many things for you like taking you and your friends to the beach and to the mall. I don't think you notice what I do for you. You just want more and more from me. I think I should take away privileges from you so then you will really know what it feels like to go without fun."

As soon as Susan hears this, she stops listening. Susan is raising a good point with her mother, but she does it in an accusatory manner, "You never let me go anywhere." When Susan learned to express her thoughts, feelings, and needs in a clear way, conversations improved.

She learned to say, "I would like to go over Diane's house. My friends spontaneously decide to meet at Diane's house after school sometimes. I want to join them, but there is no way to tell you in advance. Can I call you to let you know after I get to her house?"

Susan's mother learned to listen carefully to her daughter and validate her feelings. "I know I have been restrictive and over-protective with you. I am restrictive because I am afraid you will get hurt. But I see how much you enjoy going to see your friend. I will allow you more freedom because I see you are more mature now."

As Susan feels more successful with her mother she is able to change her thoughts about her mother to, "Mom has not been as flexible as I want, but she is now trying to grant me more freedom than I thought she could." This more reasonable attitude helped her to feel capable of working out compromises.

Mature motivation, thinking, feeling and talking avoids black and white thinking; it helps us search for the shades of gray. A father might describe a family outing in the countryside as a pleasant day with a few hitches. In contrast, his adolescent daughter might describe the same outing as "a total disaster" because a few things went wrong. The daughter might focus on the flat tire, which took 45 minutes to repair, the mosquitoes, which were abundant, and the long line in the restaurant, where the family had to wait an hour as indications that the day was unsuccessful. On the other hand, her father might feel that the tire was fixed promptly, that mosquitoes are an inevitable part of the outdoors, and that the meal was worth waiting for. The contrast between the views of father and daughter show that mature thinking can be flexible, and puts events into perspective. The father enjoyed the outing in the country because in comparison to going to work, it was fun. On the other hand the daughter had an idealized view of what the day should be like and she compared what happened to her ideal.

Another aspect of adult thinking reflected in the father's approach is a qualitative way of judging experiences. The daughter had a harder time focusing on the positive aspects of the time in the country. Rather she remembered the amount of time they had to wait and the number of things that went wrong. Adults understand that there is some good from most life experiences. Mature descriptions and dialogue reflect a search for small successes. Adolescents' thinking is concrete, less flexible and may be irreversible. The daughter pouted because she was hungry at five o'clock and wanted to eat at that moment. She was inflexible about the idea of munching on some crackers while waiting at the restaurant. The thinking of adults, and therefore their conversation, is characterized by a qualitative view of life events, a search for partial gains in experiences and an ability to apply relative standards and reversible thinking.

Below is a list of some common adolescent problems and some suggestions for how adults can counteract these self-limiting ideas through communication. Behind each one of these mistakes in thinking lies assumptions.

Goal: It is always appropriate to use considerate and polite language, but the single most important use of language is to reflect truth and reality. Thus, the young person is counseled to use language to work out honest and fair relations between people; not just say what other people want him to say.

Example:
(Two 13-year-old boys share a paper route together and they get equal money for equal work.)

Child: I have to go out and do Jon's paper route for him again today but I really don't feel like doing it. He said he had to go someplace important again but this is the third time this month! I've never asked him to do my route because I know he would get mad at me.

Parent: How do you feel?

Child: I feel mad and frustrated and caught in a bind.

Parent: How can you help yourself to feel better? I think it is important for you to pay attention to this feeling.

Child: I don't know.

Parent: This really isn't a balanced situation between you and Jon. That is probably why you feel angry. How could you make it more balanced?

Child: I could refuse to take over his route but he would be so irritated with me.

Parent: Well, think about it. Something may come up for you and you may need his help someday. Wouldn't it be ok to ask him for help?

Child: Yeah, but I don't feel like asking him.

Parent: Why not? It's good to ask friends for help, which is what he is asking you. Don't you think you could ask him to help you out when we go away next weekend?

Child: Well, I guess I'll have to ask him. I'll have to point out that I already did it for him three times, if he gets mad.

Parent: It really doesn't matter if he gets mad. What is fair is fair. You helped him three times and now you need help. So it's worth making the effort to help him when he needs it, and then feel free to ask him for help in return.

Child: Yeah and I also want to go camping next month so I'll ask him about that, too.

Some shy children and adolescents feel that they have to say the right things and accommodate other people's wishes all the time. This feeling makes them act submissive and passive. Then they are not capable of getting their own needs met. In the above example, the parent wanted to teach the child to satisfy his own needs as well as help a friend.

All of the above guidance and learning occurs through communication. Parents can convey considerable amounts of information to their older children by accepting feelings and being willing to discuss life situations. This dialogue process is vital not only because the child needs information to sort out a confusing world, but also because she will begin to learn how to counsel herself in the same way when troubles arise. You may have noticed that all of the above examples were accomplished with dialogue that went back and forth numerous times. It is tempting for adults to want to take over the conversation and lecture children. However, the child will change his thinking only when reasonable and empathic statements are made that acknowledge his feelings.

Tina made the mistake of asking her father about a movie she saw when she was about fourteen. She came home from the movies feeling happy and wanting to talk.

Tina: Dad, I just saw a movie about a law student and all the things he had to go through to find out if he was doing the right thing.

Father: That's ridiculous! Why wouldn't that be the right thing? He should just stay in school and forget about those other stupid things.

Tina: Well, I liked it because it was funny and it ended really well. He had so many problems but it all worked out.

Father: I don't have to watch movies to feel good. I live my life and have real experiences; I don't have to go watch someone else do it on a screen. What's wrong with you?

Tina: Nothing. I just liked the movie.

Father: You are a stupid girl and you'll never amount to anything. It is stupid to watch movies about stupid kids who don't know a good thing when they have it. That guy doesn't know his ass from his elbow—he should just stay in law school and shut up.

Tina's father could not understand her feelings and he was not capable of sharing her enthusiasm for the movie

He was stuck in his own rage and resentment over a student lucky enough to get into law school. Tina's father could not feel empathy for the student in the movie, nor his daughter, who so desperately wanted some acknowledgment and understanding. The conversation was disastrous for Tina, because she made herself vulnerable to her father and was then ridiculed and rejected. Let's look at the way this conversation could have gone with a parent who feels empathy for his child's feelings and concern for her ability to make decisions about her own career.

Tina: I just saw a movie about a law student and all the things he had to go through in order to find out if he was doing the right thing.

Adult: You enjoyed this movie.

Tina: I had so much fun watching it because he was so funny and full of life.

Adult: You can feel other people's happiness, can't you?

Tina: Yes, I love to get into a movie and feel for the characters.

Adult: Yeah I like that too.

Tina: I felt for his struggle because he was supposed to do just what his parents wanted him to do, but he was not sure it was the right thing for him. He took some time to do some other things and kind of got himself into some trouble.

Adult: How did you feel about the trouble he got into?

Tina: Scared. I was so worried about him and if he would be ok. I was worried that he would get into so much trouble that he would not be able to stay in law school. It was like he was going to burn his bridges behind him.

Adult: Do you ever think about that in your own life?

Tina: Yes, I know I have to get good grades so I can go to college. So I try to do well so that I give myself a chance.

Adult: I guess parents worry that kids will forget about the future and spend more time having fun. I guess parents feel like you did watching the law student wondering if he can find himself and not burn his bridges either.

Tina: Yeah, but after watching the movie I think both are important: have some fun and keep your studies going.

132

Beck, Aaron T. Cognitive Therapy and the Emotional Disorders. International Universities Press, New York, NY, 1976.

Elkind, David   Egocentrism in adolescence. Child Development, 1967, 38, 1025-1034.

Horney, Karen Self-Analysis. WW Norton and Company, New York, 1942.

SECTION III BUILDING BONDS

"For the first time in history it is possible for everyone to view the entire planet, with all its myriad, diversified peoples, in one perspective.   World peace is not only possible but inevitable."

Statement from the Universal House of Justice, October, 1985.

Chapter 13

Parents Give to Get

"I have defined love as the will to extend oneself for the purpose of nurturing one's own or another's spiritual growth. Genuine love is volitional rather than emotional. The person who truly loves does so because of a decision to love."

-Scott Peck

We know the early years are critical ones for the training and education of children. Parents have potential for growth and transformation during the early years also. Parents act as catalysts that set children in motion; children can get their parents to learn, too. Parents give to their children in order to get experience and wisdom.

My fifteen-month-old baby, Laine, stood in her crib calling "mama, mama, mama." Within the next hour, Laine and I would interact hundreds of times. I plucked her from her crib, cuddled her, and talked to her as I changed her diaper. Laine answered me by cooing, as her older brothers rushed into the room. More morning greetings and hugs passed between me, brothers, and baby. Lots of laughter, squabbling, questions, demands, and comments took place as the morning moved into action. Laine uttered one of her favorite words, "Baba." Squeals of "Baba" became more intense as Laine worked to get my attention.

Mother: Are you hungry? (puts bottle in to warm)
Child: Hungy. Baba.
   (pause)
Mother: I was busy, but I am getting your bottle now.
Child: Baba. Baba juce.
Mother: Just a minute more.
Child: Baba? (holds on mother's leg)
Mother: It's coming. The bottle's coming.
Child: (whimpers) Mama baba.
   (pause)
Mother: Yes, I'm warming your bottle. (pause) Now it's warm! Where's the top? (looks for bottle top)
Child: Baba top?
Mother: Oh, I found the bottle top. Now, here's your bottle. (gives bottle and holds her in arms)
Child: (sucks bottle) Mmmmmm.
   (pause)
Mother: Are you happy now? You were so hungry.
Child: (coos while sucking)
Mother: And thirsty too.
   (pause)
Child: Book.
Mother: Do you see a book? (looks around)
Child: Dat book.
Mother: Oh, you want to read a book while you drink!
Child: Book. Book dere. (points to table with books)
Mother: (gets the book) Here's your book.
Child: Duck. Quack quack. (looks at duck on book cover while she drinks her bottle)
Mother: Who is this? Look here. (points)
Child: Quack quack.

Mother: Yes, this duck says quack quack. But is this the Mama duck or the baby duck?
Child: Baby duck.
Mother: Yes, good girl.
Child: Baby baba.
Mother: Oh yes, the baby duck has a bottle. Just like Lainey.

This flurry of talking and activity takes about one minute. Once Laine has the bottle, there is momentary peace before she wants a book. The number of interactions that take place is remarkably high.

Exchanges between babies and their parents are universal.

When a baby does not have a parent, he is clearly at a disadvantage. Studies conducted in the 1940's and 1950's show that children raised in orphanages did not get what they needed physically, emotionally, or socially. They did not have someone to touch and hold them. They did not hear adults' voices to soothe or stimulate. They did not have an adult with whom to bond. The result was developmental delay in motivation, thinking, feeling, and talking. Physical problems involved moving, crawling, and walking. Emotional problems included listlessness, dullness, and severe depression. Social issues manifested in the inability to attach and interact with people.

The orphans ingested as many calories as home reared infants but they still did not gain weight, grow, or thrive. There was a high rate of illness and unexplained infant death.

Currently, a similar problem exists in hospitals where drug-addicted mothers give birth to addicted infants. The infants, called boarder babies, are kept in hospitals until their mother is rehabilitated. Babies are kept in crowded hospital nurseries for weeks and, sometimes, indefinitely. As in the orphanages, nurses strain to provide adequate physical care for these sick babies. The drug-addicted babies need more medical care and nurturing than non-addicted babies.

During infancy and the preschool years, children have trouble waiting their turn. When a toddler wants to be held, he is not able to wait. They are not good at postponing their needs, particularly their need to talk. There is not a lot of peace and quiet when caring for young children. Their need for care and talk seem to flow steadily all day long. Like any other work, taking care of children means being attentive, problem solving, settling disputes, negotiating schedules, initiating activities, and more. Parents are usually ready to chat, to console, to explain, to reassure, to comfort, and to play.

Whether a young child attends day care or is raised at home, it is helpful to be on the lookout for a rich and rewarding language environment. When a child is raised at home, there is usually enough time for the parent to explain and converse with the child throughout the day. Whether a parent is sorting laundry or reading a book, he is ready for exchanging questions and comments. In quality day care settings, teachers are trained in language development and understand that children need structured teaching as well as time for spontaneous dialogue. Great variations exist in the quality of day care. In choosing a day care center, it is important to evaluate the language program.

One revealing study looked at the amount of language interaction day care teachers provided for preschool children. Day care centers were studied by watching what the teachers did and observing the children's behavior. The results of the study showed that the higher quality day care centers had teachers who talked more to children. There was an emphasis on language learning where the children talked to the adults, the adults knew how to answer and encourage talk, and there was reading books and story telling. The children performed better on many different tests of intelligence as well as language development.

The low quality day care centers did not build language learning into the daily routine; the adults did not talk as much to the children, nor did they assist children in their own conversation. There was significantly less attention paid to reading books. Consequently, the children from the low quality day cares learned less language and scored lower on general measures of intelligence.

If Tina could have talked to her parents when she was a child, she might have been able to ask them to change. These changes would certainly have benefited each of her parents also.

Adult: Tina, what would you like to ask your parents?

Tina: I would like to ask them to stop fighting. They say mean things to each other, they hit, and they yell. My mother cries for a long time.

Adult: What would you like to ask of your father? What do you think he could do to make things better for you?

Tina: I want to ask him not to be so mean. I want him to know how much it hurts me when he is mean to me, my sisters, and my mother.

Adult: So you are hurt by his meanness? Is there anything else?

Tina: I want to ask him not to brag, exaggerate, and lie so much because I am embarrassed when he says things that are not true. He tells lies to make him seem better and more important than he is. I like him just the way he is but without the meanness and the lies.

Adult: It is hard to find the parts of him that you can like. The meanness and the lying must be hard for you. I worry that you might feel mean inside because of his mean treatment and that you might want to tell lies like he does.

Tina: Yes, sometimes I do and I do not like that. I know it is not right to be mean or to lie.

Adult: How about your mother? Is there something that you would change about her?

Tina: My mother lets my father treat me badly. She does not seem to care. I want my mother to say, "STOP THAT RIGHT NOW" when my father is mean to us. My mother is mean to me in quiet ways. She says mean things about people even if those people are nice to me.

Adult: So you know that there are areas where your parents

139

need to improve. If you could talk to them, would you be able to find a way to express these thoughts?

Tina: Yes, to my father I would say, "Daddy, it makes me so sad when you are mean. You can just talk to me about my mistakes instead of make me feel so bad inside. I feel that you hate me, I feel that you hate all people, and I feel that most people hate me. Is this all because you feel so bad inside too?"

Adult: You have hit on something that is true. People who act mean feel bad inside and they were treated mean when they were young. They are having trouble working out their thoughts and feelings and learning a better way to talk and express themselves. What about your mother? What would you say to her?

Tina: I would say this to my mother, "Mommy, you seem to care more about Daddy than me. I do not seem to be important to you. I feel like a worthless person who drains you and annoys you. It seems like you think I am mean, devious, and spiteful because you tell me I am mean, devious, and spiteful. It convinces me that this is true. Maybe somebody told you this about yourself; maybe you feel this way too."

Adult: Yes, Tina, your mother attributes those motives to you probably because she was accused in the same way and came to believe it too.

Tina knew about her parents' issues at a young age. Her parents mocked her, intimidated her, and failed to listen to what might have helped her grow. If we listen to our children we can learn about ourselves from them. Parenting is a two-way street. Parents give their children material and emotional support, and children give back.

Baby monkeys reared without mothers are aggressive, mean, and irritable. They cannot comprehend normal social hierarchies, they cannot make friends, nor can they mate. They are terrified of physical contact. Female monkeys, that had been reared without mothers, were artificially inseminated and delivered healthy newborns. Would motherhood help the deprived female develop social behavior and overcome her problems? The babies were mistreated by their deprived mothers and some of them died. A few baby monkeys survived by clinging to their mother's chest where they could breast-feed and stay out of harm.

The mother monkeys began to overcome their aversion to touching and contact by allowing their baby monkeys to cling and nurse. If the baby lived for the first few days, the mother would continue to feed him. They became more able to tolerate closeness and contact with their babies. By learning about infant care, the unhealthy adult monkeys transferred some of these newly acquired social behaviors to other adult monkeys. They learned to touch and some of them learned to mate after they had spent time with their "therapeutic" babies.

"Even more striking was the caretaking behavior of these monkeys when they had a second baby. It was indistinguishable from that of their nondeprived peers. They had recovered normal social functioning" (Cole, 1989).

This discovery pointed to some help for troubled adolescents. Young, healthy children were taken care of for periods of time by adolescents with social adjustment problems. Adults carefully monitored interactions between the children and youth.

Annie, age sixteen, talked about her feelings of caring for young children. Annie had never met her father and when she was born to her 48-year-old mother, all of her eight stepbrothers and sisters had grown up and moved out of the house. Annie was alone with a mother who worked 40 plus hours per week, was growing tired, and was prone to abusive and violent outbursts. Annie was emotionally about five years old as well as being exceptionally bright.

Annie: I just don't see why Justin (age 3) has to climb to the top of the fort and jump off so many times. He thinks he's

141

superman or something. Why can't he do it two or three times and then give it up?

Teacher: Remember what we were saying about repetition? You know kids have to do things many, many times in order to learn. Sounds like Justin can get to you.

Annie: I help him get up and then I have to hold his hands while he jumps down or he's gonna kill himself on all those blocks all over the sides. Then I tell him, "OK, one more time and that's all," so we do it and then I walk away. I turn around one minute later and he is standing up there again about to fall and crack his skull.

Teacher: What do you feel? When you see that he did not listen to you and that he is going to fall?

Annie: Really pissed off. But also scared—he's gonna crash.

Teacher: So the thought inside your mind may be, "He is so bad for not listening to me, but he is gonna get hurt." Then the feeling is being mad and scared.

Annie: Yeah. So but, I run over to him and help him down. My mother would've whipped my butt.

Teacher: What would have been better for you?

Annie: Well, you know all this talkin' and tryin' to understand feelins. I feel all burning inside and like I just want to burn his britches.

Teacher: But Annie, you have never done that here in the child-care program.

Annie: No, because it's not right. I do what you all have been saying. I get burning mad and then I look for the thoughts that are makin' me mad. I think, "You no-good brat" then I try to change it to "You just a kid and you need to do things a hundred times to get it right. You just on number fifty now. I can help you down."

Teacher: Sounds right to me. Must be specially hard for you because nobody took care of you that way.

After a period of time caring for the young children, the adolescents understood what they were expected to do with the children. They developed empathy. There was marked improvement in the youths' ability to get along with their peers and families. Nurturing the young requires a person to extend himself beyond his own needs. People (and monkeys) make efforts to help the helpless. This process seems to make healing and growing possible.

Clarke-Stewart, K. Alison Infant day care: maligned or malignant. American Psychologist, 1989, 44(2), 266-273.

Cole, M. and Cole, S. The Development of Children. W.H. Freeman and Company, New York, 1989.

Furman, W., Rahe, D.E. and Hartup, W.W. Rehabilitation of socially withdrawn preschool children. Child Development, 1986, 50, 4, 915-922.

McCartney, Kathleen Effect of the Quality of Day Care on Children's Language Development. Developmental Psychology, 1984. 20. 244-260.

Peck, Scott The Road Less Traveled. Simon and Schuster, New York, 1978.

Pinneau, S.F. The infantile disorders of hopitalism and anaclytic depression. Psychological Bulletin, 1955, 52, 429-452.

Schaffer, R. Mothering. Harvard University Press, Cambridge, Massachusetts, 1979.

Spitz, R.A. Unhappy and fatal outcomes of emotional deprivation and stress in infancy. In I. Galdston, ed., Beyond the Germ Theory. Health Education Council, 1954, 120-131.

Chapter 14

Listen To Me, Mom and Dad

"Oh my friends, listen with hearts and souls to the songs of the spirit."

-Baha'u'llah

How can we tell if someone is a good communicator? A good communicator must be able to speak well, but even more important, he must also be able to listen. When we talk, our blood pressure increases significantly compared to times when we listen. When we listen, our blood pressure drops. Some physicians recommend that patients with hypertension increase the amount of time they spend listening to help decrease their blood pressure.

How do we know what to say and who to say it to? How do we learn about listening and who to listen to? Children gradually, with patient training, discriminate what kind of talk is acceptable with different kinds of people. A young girl will eventually realize that Daddy may want to know that she just got new socks but that the mailman will not be interested.

Listening-talk is the ability to listen, then summarize what you've heard. Sometimes it helps to say, "I hear you saying...." You would be surprised at how often intelligent, caring parents and spouses cannot repeat what their child or spouse has just said using different words, but the same meaning. Even more often, children have a hard time paraphrasing what their parents say. Parents who paraphrase have children who are also better at it. First, paraphrasing is important because it is a confirmation. Second, listening is a way to tell a person that you value his or her ideas. It is like saying, "I believe your thoughts have merit."

In therapy sessions with families, it is important for the therapist to ask people if they understood the speaker, and if they would summarize what he or she said. The therapist helps the listener hear the message the speaker is trying to send.

Sue   (an eight-year-old): Dad said I could turn the TV on and he said I could have a snack. So when Mom comes home she shouldn't yell at me if the TV is on and I am eating. It's not fair. I'm always getting yelled at even when I am doing what Dad said I can do. Mom just wants everything to be her way and she wants to yell at me for no good reason.

Mom: I have a good reason to yell at you because you never listen to a thing I say.

Me: Mom, I am wondering if you heard what Sue said. Would you paraphrase what Sue said before we go on?

Mom: Sue is saying that she just wants to do what she wants. When she gets home from school she wants to watch TV and have her snack in the living room. She doesn't care that I don't allow that. And she does not clean up after herself.

Me: I did not get that. Let's check it out with Sue. Did your Mom get it right?

Sue: No, Dad said I could watch TV and have my snack. He

said it was OK and you yelled at me anyway.

Me: Can you try it again, Mom?

Mom: I don't care if Dad said you could watch TV and have your snack, I said you can't.

Me: That's closer. I think Sue is saying that she wants to watch TV and have a snack. Because she got her father to say yes, she thinks its OK. She does not think it is fair that you yell at her when Dad said it was OK. How does that sound to you Sue?

Sue: Yes, that's it.

Mom was so upset by Sue's conduct that she did not focus on the idea that Sue thinks it is acceptable to disobey if she can get her father to agree. Mom would have done better if she said, "I hear you saying that Dad said you could eat and watch TV, so you did it." When Mom paraphrased Sue's message, she could then understand the problem. The problem was problematic communication between Mom and Dad. Nothing is more difficult than listening with an open mind when we are upset. We focus on our own point of view and arguments and meanwhile it is hard to listen and understand. Only when we stop and listen, paraphrase accurately and make sure we understand can the talk stay on track.

The second survival skill for listening includes one simple sentence. It is, "Tell me your thoughts and feelings," and it is a listening-invitation that means I am ready to hear you. When we stop, put aside our own needs and listen, then we are communicating. This is crucial for parents to do with their children in order to help them feel heard, recognized, and understood. If we give our partner the floor and let him express his thoughts and feelings then listening has begun. There are a variety of ways to say, "Tell me your thoughts and feelings."

Listening Invitations

I want to listen to what you have to say.
I am interested in your thoughts and feelings.
Will you tell me what's on your mind?
I want to understand your ideas.
I want to know how you came to those conclusions.
I would like to know more about what you just said.
Would you share your reasoning with me?
A penny for your thoughts.
I care about what is going on inside you, want to talk?
Explain more about that.
Talk to me.

There are many ways to let a person know you want to listen to him. Listening and using one's knowledge, caring, and experience to understand validates children's sense of themselves. It is not easy to listen for the sake of another person because we have our own feelings and ideas to express. But the ability to listen to another person is at the heart of good communication. How else can we genuinely understand another person's point of view?

Active listening, like jogging, requires stamina. Not only is talking recognized as activity, but we know listening requires the same kind of mental exertion. Listening means we are able to be attentive and hear what the other person is saying while, at the same time are trying to feel what the other person is feeling. Listening and talking are not like watching television. The intellectual and social skills involved in conversation can be improved and sharpened.

Active listening is not silence, although that is one part of it. We have seen that two essential skills for active listening include listening-talk and listening invitations. When listening is going well, empathy is shared. Consider the feelings of a five-year-old girl whose two cantankerous parents have gone through a long divorce. I am trying to listen, for Ellie's sake, and show her the empathy that I feel. At the same time, I am helping her to become aware of her own power so she can make an effort to control her own life.

Ellie: My Mom has a picture of me on her refrigerator. We hang all my pictures up there.

Me: On the refrigerator door?

Ellie: Yes. When I come home from school I put my papers right up near my picture. Then everyone can see it and my Mom can see it.

Me: You put your school papers near the photograph of you?

Ellie: Right around it, like a circle. And it has my Mom, too. And we were at the zoo. But Dad was not there, it was just me and Mom. But Dad has a picture of me too.

Me: Did your Dad take that picture of you?

E: Nooo! Mom takes all the pictures. She has a camera and she always takes pictures. Even at her work. She takes lots of pictures. (pause) Dad has our picture near his bed. It's a picture of him and me. On the table. We look at it before I go to bed at his house.

Me: Your Dad probably likes to look at your picture before he goes to sleep. Do you like to think of your Dad before you go to sleep?

E: Yeah, I like Dad but Dad and Mom fight all the time.

Me: How do you feel about that?

E: Bad. I don't like it. They should stop fighting.

Me: Do they fight now?

E: Ummmm. Not as much. I have lots of pictures in the big book at Mom's house....like when I was a baby. Mommy and Daddy were both holding me.

Me: You like to look at pictures of both Mommy and Daddy holding you?

E: Daddy is not going to come back home. He has his own house.

Me: It must be sad for you, Ellie. Want to tell me how you feel?

E: I really want my Mommy and Daddy and me to live together again. I don't know why they can't love each other anymore. I love them and I try to make them love each other.

Me: Want to talk about how you try to get your Mom and Dad together?

E: I try to get them to talk. I try to tell them the good things that each of them does for me.

Me: Is it working?

E: No. They still fight. My Mom still cries.

Me: Do you still hope that your Mommy and Daddy will change their minds?

E: Yes. I want Daddy to come home but I know my Mommy doesn't want him to come back. I don't know what to do—I feel so bad. (cries)

Me: I can see how sad you are.

E: (nods her head yes)

Me: You know you cannot change what your Mom and Dad decide to do but you might be able to think of some things you can do to feel better.

E: Nothing can make me feel better.

Me: You like pictures just like your Mommy and Daddy do. Maybe if you could have pictures of Mommy and Daddy to keep that would make you feel better.

E: I don't know.

Me: You can't make your Mommy and Daddy be together but you can put pictures together any way you want them to be.

E: Yeah, I could have a picture of Mommy, one of Daddy and one of me. I could keep them with me at Mommy's house then I could carry them to Daddy's house. I could arrange them any way I want them to be.

Me: Could you ask your mother for a picture of herself and you, then ask your Dad for a picture of him?

E: Yeah.

Me: How would you feel about that?

E: Good. Maybe Mommy would let me use her old camera to take the pictures myself. She lets me take pictures sometimes, you know.

Me: That's great. I like your idea about taking pictures.

Talking can help children gain control of their world. Through language children can express their needs, influence people, get parents to pay attention, and make changes. Learning to ride a bike takes practice, and so does talking and listening. The more children are encouraged to talk and express what is inside of them, the more practice they will have in gaining control of their environment. We want children to feel as though they can master the art of self-expression and negotiation. None of this can happen without someone who is willing to listen to them.

Giglioli, Pier Paolo (ed) Language and Social context. Penguin Books, New York, 1972.

Lerner, Harriet Goldhor   The Dance of Intimacy. Harper and Row, Publishers, New York, NY, 1989.

Searle, J. What is a Speech Act? In Language and Social Context, Giglioli, P.P., Penguin Books, New York, 1972.

Chapter 15

Girl Talk, Boy Talk

"Parents are caretakers not only of their offspring, but also -in a more primordial, phyletic sense- of the germ plasma and the genetic code. "

-John Money

About twenty-five years ago when I was a graduate student, I sat, fascinated, watching a group of preschool children jumping, running, chasing, throwing, talking, yelling, and listening. I could not help from noticing that the boys were behaving differently from the girls. Some of the language and behavioral differences between the boys and the girls were striking. I was conducting a study on conversational congruence in children's language development but I was continually distracted by the differences between the boys and the girls. At the time, I had no idea that girls' talk would be systematically different from boys' talk, but the behavior before my eyes made me suspicious.

When I was watching the children in my study playing, I noticed that the girls would say something like, "look at this house I b..." and before she got to finish her sentence a boy would come by with a truck and yell, "Zoooooom", right in front of her face to call attention to his toy and to try to get the girl to play with him. During one play sequence a girl and boy played with puppets by holding up their puppets alternately and making them give a speech. When the boy spoke the girl mainly listened to him because, as she said, "You're supposed to listen to the puppet." But when she made her puppet speak, the boy held up his puppet, broke into her speech and said, "Hello" numerous times and then laughed. The girls in these two examples did not seem to mind the boys' behavior, perhaps because both girls felt free to tell the boys how they felt about it. "Go zoooom somewhere else," the first girl finally declared and the second girl continued to insist, "You're supposed to listen to the puppet when he gives a speech!"

I collected language samples of many pairs of children in girl-girl, girl-boy and boy-boy combinations all playing and talking freely for about an hour. I looked at my data to see if there were differences between the three types of pairs. There were. Guess which pair showed the greatest numbers of interruptions and intrusions into the other person's talk? Interruptions were defined as instances of overlapping speech where one person breaks off another person's ongoing sentence.

The girl-boy pairs showed the greatest numbers of intrusions and interruptions. My initial hunch proved right; boys are barging in on girls' talk significantly more often than girls are doing this to boys. Essentially I found that girls interrupted each other the least frequently and that boys interrupt boys sometimes. But the point is, put boys and girls together and this brings out the most interruptions.

It is as if girls are playing and talking according to some covert rules of politeness that say 1) try to go along with one another's talk and play or 2) if you really want to break into someone else's talk and play do it carefully so as to blend it in and avoid being intrusive or forceful. Thus the girls' talk appears to be careful and caring while the boys' talk looks more rough and rugged. Vivian Gussin Paley, a kindergarten teacher, wrote about the same kind of observation she made in her classroom.

Janie runs out of the doll corner shouting, "I'm telling!" She finds me at the sink. "Me and Mary Ann and Charlotte and Karen were playing in there and they came in and started shooting!"

Mary Ann is at her side now and adds her own complaints: "They spoiled everything. Andrew was where we put the clothes and Jeremy was on top of the refrigerator and Paul stuck his fingers in my face."

The boys are still in the doll corner. "What were you playing, Andrew?" I ask.

"Cops and robbers."

"In the doll corner?"

"We need to steal food. And also gold. Because we're the bad guys. We're robbers."

"Well, you can't play it in the doll corner. Play it outside, later."

"Can't we do it in the blocks?"

"No. No shooting. That's only for outside."

(Paley, pg. ix)

In this passage, Vivian Gussin Paley captures the rough and rugged style of the boys as they play cops and robbers by breaking into the girls' orderly game of house. The girls do not want the intrusion of cops and robbers into the game of house because the boys are not careful and caring in their talk and play. The girls know how to take care of themselves and get their needs met by using their careful and caring style with the teacher. They know their teacher will stop the boys in their tracks and they know how to get the teacher to do it all in a polite and systematic way.

Robin Lakoff, a linguist, has suggested that women are the "repositories of tact" and that women abide by rules of politeness, courtesy and manners to a greater extent than men in conversation. Perhaps preschool girls have learned something of this already in that they seem to abide by the politeness rule that goes like this, "Do not speak until it is your turn, wait until the other person has finished talking and then begin your turn." Or when it comes to undesirable intrusions into their games, girls politely explain to an adult what the boys did wrong knowing that the adult will right the wrong. In this way the girls show equal competence at getting their needs met but they do it in a careful and caring way.

Girls talk in a way that looks more careful and caring while boys talk in a way that is more rough and rugged. Could it be that looks deceive? Even though boys look more rough and rugged, could it be that they are concerned and considerate too? And although girls look more careful and caring, could it be that they are hardy and tough also? Two kindergarten children are playing on a mat; they have known each other for about six months as classmates.

Beth: I'm going to do a somersault, you wait, then after me, you can go. (does a somersault by rolling over him)

Randy: Watch this! (flings his body across her path)

Beth: Hey, you were supposed to wait for your t....

Randy: Let's do that again! You start to roll and I'll flop down under you!

Beth: Ok, but don't go until say so. Ready, set, g...

Randy: Here I go!!!

Beth wants Randy to take turns doing somersaults on a mat but Randy has a different idea. He does not want to wait for his turn at somersaults, nor does he wait for his turn at talk. He flops down across Beth's path as she somersaults and then he interrupts her verbal protest. Randy seems to want to play with Beth but he does not want to adhere to her timing or discuss her ideas about the play; he feels free to do and say what he wants, when he wants. On the other hand, Beth also wants to play with Randy but she wants him to discuss their play and come to some agreement on what they will do. For example Beth wants to talk over whether or not one person somersaults at a time, who says when to go, and what action they will perform before they do it. When Randy does not want to do what Beth wants by discussing the play, Beth seems able to go with his flow but she does not stop trying to talk about the play.

Look at this one small exchange between Beth and Randy

taken out of the play scene described above. Now that you know what was happening between them, you will be able to understand some of the details of this one brief interchange.

TALK

Beth: Hey, you were supposed to wait for your t.....

Randy: Let's do that again! You start to roll and I'll flop down under you.

FEELINGS

I feel some frustration because he is not talking to me and he interrupted me. But that was fun and I feel like doing it again. I feel excited that we could do this together.

I feel that was fun to do with Beth. I feel enthusiastic and I want to do it again. I want to just burst out with the feeling that I want to do it again. I don't feel like waiting or talking.

THOUGHTS

I think that when we are playing together, Randy should talk to me about his moves. I think it is good to wait for your turn.

I think that was a good trick when Randy flopped under me.

I think I should be able to finish my sentences.

I think that was a good trick. I think we can do that again even better. I think I can judge when to flop in.

I think all her talking takes away from the fun.

MOTIVATION

I like Randy. I want to be friends. I want to play in a fair way with him. I want to cooperate and I want him to cooperate with me.

I like Beth. I want to have fun with her and I want to be friends. I want to do what I like to do. I want her to do what she wants too.

It is obvious that I have extrapolated in my interpretations of

Beth and Randy's motivation, thinking, and feeling. I took liberties with these interpretations in order to make two points. The first point is that from talk, we cannot always know exactly what the other person means to imply or what they feel. Beth may appear to be bossy and Randy may appear to be callous if you take their talking styles literally. But when you examine their motivation, thinking and feeling neither of them seem bossy or callous, they seem like genuine and amiable human beings. I picked out this example and extrapolated to their motivations, thoughts, and feelings because I know this to be true of these two children and I believe the motivations, thinking, and feeling I have described to be true for most people, most of the time.

The second point I tried to bring out using the Beth and Randy example is that boys and girls, like men and women, have different styles of talk. I want to describe in more detail what we know about masculine and feminine language styles based on research findings. I believe that by pointing to some differences in the way that girls and boys talk we will not misconstrue this to mean one is better than the other, just different and complementary.

Some old research, done in the 1950's, was flawed and it led us to believe that boys learn language later than girls, boys are less competent linguistically, and score lower on test of language development. This is a confusing area because some reports do show sex differences on language development while many measures show no differences. We do know that sex differences in language development are not as clear cut as what was once thought. We know now that girls and boys learn to talk at about the same rates but that there are significant differences in the ways they use what they know about language; boys use talk in a rough and ready way, while girls tend to be careful and caring. These different language styles may have thrown people off track to misperceive boys' language style as being less advanced. Below is a list of some of the differences in the way that boys and girls talk

GIRLS' TALK: CAREFUL and CARING

1. The purpose of girls' talk seems to be to create intimacy and connections between people.

Elaine (age 5): Do you want to play with me? Look I can make room for you right here. (she moves over for Ann)

Ann (age 6): Ok, I will play with you because it's not dinner time yet. My Mom is going to call me at six o'clock.

Elaine: Good, then you can stir this soup. It looks good, doesn't it? (looks up at Ann)

Elaine is going to encourage Ann to come and play with her by explicitly asking her to come play and by stating that she will move for Ann's sake. After Ann agrees to play, Elaine immediately says what Ann can do to join her play and then asks Ann a question to draw her into the talk and play.

2. Girls create intimacy in talk by orienting their body toward their friend, maintaining eye-contact during talk, and letting the friend speak without interrupting her.

Elaine: (sitting in the sand)

Ann: (standing) Oh yes. But how about making a mud pie? I can make it in this pail? But where can we get some water? (says this while bending down to look right at Elaine)

Elaine: My mother said it is ok to turn the hose on. Want me to get it for you? (looks up at Ann)

Ann: Yeah. Then we can make a river too. Do you want to make a river? (girls look at each other as they walk over to hose)

Ann orients her body and her eyes toward Elaine even though one is sitting and the other is standing. The girls maintain eye contact and body orientation even as they both get up to get the hose. They allow each other to complete their turn before beginning to speak and they acknowledge what the other has said.

Girls seem to do this in order to provide continual feedback to their speaker that they are attentive and care about the other person's feelings. It appears that girls speak in this way to create closeness and intimacy.

3. Girls use talk to make friends and nurture their friendships along; talking is an important part of girls' play.

Elaine: I was sad yesterday when you were playing with Karen. I wanted to talk to you.

Ann: You can come over even if I am playing with Karen. We can all play house together. I was the mother, Karen was the child yesterday.

Elaine: But Karen doesn't talk to me sometimes.

Ann: She is grouchy sometimes. I will tell her to talk to you and then she will. If she doesn't then she'll have to be the father and you can be the child. (girls do not want to be the father when playing house—that is a low status position for them)

Elaine felt left out of the other girls' play the previous day and she is testing the waters to see if Ann cares about her feelings. Ann tries to reassure her by talking to her and she shows her allegiance to Elaine by her willingness to put Karen in the one-down position of father. Ann responds to Elaine's concern by talking which creates a bond and intimacy between the two girls.

4. Girls talk to their friends as they play in order to maintain a connection with them. They also talk to their friends in order to encourage them and support them. Girls use more questions, more rising intonations that sound like questions and more tag questions than do boys. Girls use these questions to continually acknowledge their listener and encourage her to participate. Also, as girls play together they call out to one another what they are doing as a way to stay connected and maintain intimacy.

Elaine: Let's make a bridge over this river. Do you want to start on that side? I will start over here. This is going to be a great bridge!

Ann: Yeah, I'll start on that side but I need more sand. I'm going to get some from under the slide? Look, here is the sand.

Elaine: Good. This side looks low. Is it low? Should I build it up now?

Ann: Yes, for sure. Let's dig down farther because there is not enough room under the bridge. Maybe I will dig over here?

Much of what the girls are doing does not have to be spoken aloud. But they enjoy calling out what they are doing in order to keep the talk going. By keeping the talk going they feel connected with the other. They use questions not so much to get information but to get confirmation that their partner is with them. Elaine asks if Ann want to start building the bridge on one side while she announces she will start on the other side. The purpose of this question is more to keep Ann involved than to obtain a fact. Ann makes a statement but uses a rising intonation that sounds like a question as she gets some sand from under the slide. Likewise, Elaine knows that her side is low but she asks if Ann thinks it is low before she starts to build it up.

5. Girls tend to soften their talk in consideration of other people's feelings. They make fewer direct requests like "Give me the ball," instead they might say, "Let's share the ball." They do not like confrontation or fights because that would compromise their intimacy and friendship. Girls allow flexible rules, more compromising and more evasion which preserves the harmony. Their goal in conversation is to be liked and accepted.

Karen: (age 5, runs over to where the girls are playing) Can I play with you?

Ann: Sure, we're making a river with a bridge.

Elaine: You can work on my side. I need lots more sand over

here. Want to help me get it?

Karen: Yeah, I'll help you get it. Where's a pail for me?

Ann: You have to get one from the garage. (pause) But maybe you can share mine with me?

Karen: How about I'll use yours when you don't need it, then I'll use Elaine's when she is not using it?

Elaine: That's a good idea. Here. (hands her the pail)

Ann: This river needs some more water?

Karen: But this side will fall down if we put water in the river now.

Ann: First, let's all fix it, then we'll put the water in.

Elaine: I'll get the water ready.

Karen does not say, "Gimme your pail" but instead asks a question. Eventually Ann realizes that Karen wants a pail and she offers to share, then Karen comes up with a compromise plan about sharing the pails among all three girls and suits them all.

Notice that Elaine accepts Karen into the play and does not bring up the topic of yesterday's rejection. Evading the issue and engaging Karen in the talk and play take a higher priority.

BOYS' TALK: ROUGH and RUGGED

1. The purpose of boys' talk seems to be to maintain hierarchical social structure. Boys jockey for social status and try to maintain the one-up, one-down positions that exist.

Steve: (age 7) Hey, it's my turn! You've had a long turn. (the boys are playing on monkey bars)

Brett: (age 6) Ok, just wait a minute. (pause while he finishes his move) There. I almost got it.

Steve: That's not it! You messed up. Watch this. (he swings on bar, then flips off, lands on feet)

Brett: I can do that. Move out of the way! (swings and flips, lands on bottom)

Steve: Watch the pro. I'll show you how it's done. (does swing and flip again)

You might think that Steve is being unkind to Brett. He is not. He is a kind and thoughtful boy and his way of talking to Brett reinforces that he is one-up from Brett both in age and in gymnastic skill. He is not criticizing Brett even though it may look like it, in fact Steve is actually trying to help Brett learn to do the flip and land on his feet. Steve does not say kind and encouraging words to Brett because that would put Brett down and cast him as a baby or wimp. Instead, Steve maintains his one up position but continues to take turns with Brett and coach him on how to flip over better. This rough and rugged talking style from Steve implies that Brett will get it if he keeps trying; it is, in essence, encouragement.

2. Boys maintain social status in the hierarchy by talking in a variety of ways including giving orders, joking, sidetracking, name-calling, interrupting, challenging, boasting, arguing.

Steve: Knucklehead, that's your butt not your feet. (Brett lands on his bottom again) Let me go now. Move! (tries a move and lands on his knees)

Brett: That's your knees not your butt! (takes his turn and goes across bars skipping one bar)

Steve: Trying to show off again. You look like a monkey.

Brett: You act like one, or no maybe a gorilla. Maybe you're going to go home to the z.....

Steve: Get moving, it's my turn. Slowing up at the end?

Believe it or not, this is a friendly exchange. I witnessed this at the school playground the other day and I knew the boys. They are both considerate children and were friendly and respectful to me. Needless to say, they did not speak quite as rough and ready to me but they did speak this way to each other and the other boys. There was name-calling, boasting, challenging, interrupting, and other behaviors that serve to show social status. Steve calls Brett a monkey but when Brett calls him a gorilla, Steve puts an end to it by interrupting him.

3. Boys do not rely on talk to make friends and keep friendships going. Boys use talk to maintain their social status with their friends and they see to it that talk stays on a parallel course; they do not nurture or coddle each other in conversation because that would mean they were putting their friend in a one-down position.

Jeff: (8 years old) So what ya doing?

Steve: Doing penny flips. Can you do one?

Jeff: Oh yeah. It looks easy. (tries and lands on his bottom)

Brett: I can do it much better than that. Get out of the way. (he does a good flip and lands on his feet)

Steve: Wow! You ate your Wheaties. (laughs)

Brett: (happy with his progress) Get out of the way, I wanna try it again.

Jeff: No, it's my turn. Step aside, young man. (to Brett)

Brett: Maybe I'm younger but I can do a penny flip and you can't.

Jeff: (tries a flip, does it better but lands on his bottom) Yoooo. I almost got it.

Brett: Yeah right.

Steve: It was ok. You gotta flip with more energy. Watch the monkey. (Brett does it again correctly)

Brett: Nothing to it.

Brett is proud of his accomplishment but he does not go easy on the older, newcomer Jeff, who cannot execute a penny flip yet. Steve is still taking the role of teacher but he does not put either boy down by overtly coaxing or praising. He just continues to give feedback and correct the boys who are learning. He comes close to praising Brett when he tells him to do it again, but Steve also calls Brett "monkey" as if to deflect the praise.

4. Boys do not tend to look at each other when they talk and neither do they orient their bodies toward one another. Boys are more often moving, squirming, wiggling, and looking around as they speak

Jeff: How do you get around?

Steve: (not looking at Jeff) You gotta swing hard like this, then whip your head and shoulders down.

Brett: Then try landing on your feet. (Brett is faced away from the other boys and is hanging up side down on another bar—he laughs)

During the entire episode, the boys rarely looked at each other and most of the time they were speaking they were also moving on the monkey bars. Notice also there were no lengthy explanations or speeches, just a lot of comments and one-liners.

5.   Boys tend to express their thoughts and feelings in a straight-forward manner without softening their speech. They use directives such as "Open the window" instead of saying "It's getting warm in here, isn't it?" Their rules for conversation or games are rigid and unbending. Their goal in conversation is to preserve their status, not to soften the impact of their statements.

Jeff: Hey, I have to go in a minute. Get out of my way. (he takes a long turn)

Steve: You're bar-hogging. Give it a rest.

Jeff: One more try. (lands on his bottom)

Steve: Your flip is getting faster. Now move it.

Jeff: I gotta go, just wait. (tries again, almost stands, then falls back)

Steve: (pulls his legs) Get off.

Brett: Yeah, get off already.

Jeff: (breaks his legs free and tries once more) Almost. Gotta go, see ya.

The boys do not pull their punches. When it is their turn they might wait a minute but any more than that and they let the other boy know about it clearly. They were all good-natured about taking turns but none of them tried to please or placate the others.

There are clear differences between the way girls and boys talk. When each child is playing with same-sex friends it is easy for all involved to understand each other. But when opposite sex children play together misunderstandings may arise because of the different styles. As children grow up, they must learn to work out their differences with members of the same sex who are likely to follow more closely to their style of talking but they must also adjust to the opposite sex who may be operating by different rules. Deborah Tannen, a linguist, has written about male and female conversational differences and she points out that each sex has its own culture of sorts and the opposite sex has to figure out how the rules of this foreign culture work.

If women speak and hear a language of connection and intimacy, while men speak and hear a language of status and independence, then communication between women and men can be like cross-cultural communication, prey to a clash of conversational styles. Instead of different dialects, it has been said that they speak different genderlects. (Tannen, 1990, pg. 42)

We all want our children to fit in with other children and get along. We want them to make friends, feel bonds with other people, and become good at conversation. We have to let them speak in their own way as this is essential to their sense of being male or female. As long as the family communication remains encouraging and caring, then adjustments we make in listening to and speaking with our boys and girls will pay off.

Coates, Jennifer Women, Men and Language. Longman Press, London and New York, 1986.

Esposito (Remig), Anita Sex Differences in Children's Conversation. Language and Speech, 22, 213-220, 1979.

Goodwin, M.H. Directive-response speech sequences in girls' and boys' task activities, pg 157-73 in McConnell-Ginet et al (eds) Women and Language in Literature and Society, Praeger, New York, 1980.

Lakoff, Robin Language and Women's Place. Harper and Row, New York, 1975.

Macaulay, Ronald K. The Myth of Female Superiority in Language. Journal of Child Language, 5, 353-363, 1978.

Money, John and Ehrhardt, Anke A. Man and Woman, Boy and Girl. The John Hopkins University Press, Baltimore, 1972.

Paley, Vivian Gussin Boys and Girls, Superheroes in the Doll corner. The University of Chicago Press, Chicago, 1984.

Sheldon, Amy Pickle Fights: Gendered Talk in Preschool Disputes. Discourse Processes, 13:1.

Tannen, Deborah You Just Don't Understand, women and Men in Conversation. Ballentine Book, New York, 1990.

:

Chapter 16

Single Parent's Talk

"...Genuine assertiveness is a means of establishing equality in a relationship. " (Alberti and Emmons, p.195)

Going it alone, although a challenge, is sometimes best for all. If a single parent can maintain positive and forthright communication with her children, her relatives, community contacts, ex-husband, and ex-relatives, then she is going to be able to cope. Raising children can be difficult; raising children without a helping partner can be even more so. The solutions to most problems for single parents will come in the form of getting help through speaking up, speaking out, and speaking calmly.

Single parent families can be close, loving, and bonded together like any other family. To understand that single parent families are families indeed, let's define the term "family." A family is made up of different patterns of adults and children. A family can include two adults, for instance a mother and a grandmother, or a mother and a father. A family can be headed by one adult, perhaps a grandmother alone or a father alone. Children are present in a family whether they are young or old, biological or adopted, stepsiblings, or cousins. There can be one child or ten children in a family such that any combination of an adult and a child constitutes a family.

There have been negative connotations associated with single-parent families. Words like broken-families, partial families, reconstituted families, incomplete families, and divorced families all have a less than positive connotation. These terms conjure up images of families that have failed, that have been defeated, and that have deficits and that is not fair.

The United States Bureau of Census has identified four descriptions of families: divorced, separated, widowed and never married. To this list add two parent families of the same gender. Some types of families come about from change within a two-parent nuclear family while other families began as single-parent families. Many situations cause families to take on different forms. Consider an adult who leaves the family for an extended military service, an adult who commutes long distances, an adult who lives away for long periods of time for job reasons, an adult who is in a medical facility for a prolonged course of treatment, or an adult who is incarcerated.

The statistics about single-parent families' occurrence have changed a great deal over the last three decades. In the 1990's, 90% of all single-parent households are presently headed by a woman. Further, 90% of children of color and 60% of white children will spend some of their time in a single-parent household. Ninety percent of all children living in single-parent homes will live below (or right around) the poverty line. The median earnings for single-mother families was approximately $9000 in the late 1980's while the median earning for a husband-wife headed household was $32,000.

That 90% of single mothers and children live in poverty or near-poverty is a shameful fact about our society. Women face discrimination in society, at their jobs, in the housing market, in financial institutions, in education, in relationships, and in family life. They are not given equal status with men in society at large, they are not promoted along with men at work, and not given equal pay. They are discriminated against in the housing market because most landlords prefer two-parent families. They are discriminated against in schools where teachers rate their children as worse off once they know about their single-parent status. In relationships, women still take a one down position with men, and in family life most women now work a second shift after they get home from their job.

One woman, Rita, spoke to me about her experiences after she was separated from her husband. She had two young children.

Me: Can you tell me why you came here today?

Rita: Well, my husband has been abusive with me and the kids all along and we had a bad fight about two months ago, in July, and he left that night really mad. He has never come home again to live although he has seen the children. Now it is September and I cannot pay the rent because I have very little money. I'm worried about the children. We have so many problems. (she begins to cry)

Me: It sounds like you have been trying to hold on.

Rita: I work in a laundry and dry cleaning store, I work full-time and I make minimum wage. My husband has not given me any money. After I pay for my child-care I don't have enough money for food and rent.

Me: Can you find an apartment with lower rent?

Rita: I looked at an apartment that had two rooms and was much less money than what I pay now. I liked it and I told the landlord that I would take it and that I would bring the deposit to him the next day. I mentioned that my children and I could put our things in here easily. When I went to see him the next day, he said he had rented the apartment to a young couple because he thought they were more suitable. I just went home and cried.

Me: Rita, do you have any one that will help you? Do you have friends or family?

Rita: My parents do not help me. My brothers live far away. I have a few friends from work. My husband comes around to see the children every three weeks or so. But he says he does not have any money. I don't know what to do.

Research studies have shown that single-parents are more

168

likely to seek help from other people and agencies than are individuals from two-parent families. This fact has been used against single women to show that they are less capable and more dependent. The opposite is true. When a single parent remains alone and avoids help from social agencies, community organizations, churches, and friends the problems start to pile up. Single mothers who utilize whatever social agencies and community programs are available, tend to get more for themselves and their children. I am advocating for single mothers to talk to people about their problems and their children's needs in order to benefit from community resources until they can provide for their children. Communication is key. I am not advocating dependence on the welfare system or abdication of personal responsibility. I am encouraging single parents to get help with social, psychological, and financial problems so that their children have an optimal chance to grow. I am advocating for single mothers to continue to work as hard as they can each day at their jobs, at work, and home.

A single mother I know as a client was forced to leave her job of five years in October. I knew her from previous counseling and I believe she is a hard worker and a good worker. She has three children and presently she has no income. She decided to use every opportunity to get what her children need and her goal is to find another job to support her children. Her first smart move was to take her job dispute to a state agency, which has supported her in filing a racial discrimination charge. She was told by a lawyer that she has a good case because he has substantial evidence to back up her claim of racial discrimination. Her next move was to get some medical coverage for herself and her children during this period of time and to get psychotherapy for herself and the child who needs it. Her last goal, as it gets close to the end of November, was to put her children's names into a Christmas charity drive. This last step was the hardest for her because she had always put together a wonderful holiday season for her children all on her own. She overcame her own frustration and anger in order to talk to the people who run the charity drive. She explained the ages and needs of each child in a clear and straightforward way, got past her anger, and the children enjoyed Christmas.

Single-parents need to talk to other people about their children and about their own life. We all need support in parenting and single parents must be creative in searching it out. There are parenting classes offered through schools, hospitals, and government agencies. Make calls and find out about them; they are an invaluable resource for all parents. There are many support groups offered in communities for women and for mothers from local safe houses, women's organizations, and church support groups. Find a group, grit your teeth, and walk in. That's the hardest part. Stay and listen to other people talk about parenting and family life. If we don't search out means for communicating with other people about what we are going through, we will be all alone with it. That is too hard for any one.

Single parenting requires one person to do a great deal of work including physical maintenance, emotional nurturing, helping with school work, encouraging a social life, building a spiritual foundation, guidance, and discipline. Seeking help, looking for support, and actively engaging community programs are healthy coping mechanisms in dealing with all the aspect of parenting. Trying to go it alone or taking the "supermom" or "superdad" role will only lead to failure and frustration because it is an impossible standard. Being supermom is lonely and it tends to alienate mothers keeping them at home fighting their battles single-handedly. Rather, when a single mother begins to look for help, problem-solve, and delegate responsibility, then she has a chance of getting more assistance and more services for herself and her children. Social services departments, town recreational departments, church groups, YMCA and YWCA, support groups, big brother/big sister programs, volunteer tutors, counseling, and the like are all potential sources of support.

The thinking-feeling-talking cycle is useful here in problem solving single-parenting issues. Let's first look at some thoughts that empower single parents to search out the best for their children and themselves.

Thoughts for Healthy Parenting
1. Asking for help and being able to accept help is one hallmark of a mature adult.
2. Taking control of what happens to me and my children is a sign of self-confidence. If I make plans to talk to other parents or take a class, then I will have more information to rely upon. If I choose to sign my kids up for social skills groups at the YWCA, then my kids will learn and grow.
3. More social skills and better ability to communicate can be learned at any time by any person. I can begin to learn more now. If I need some counseling, I will get it. If I need to read a book, I will make the time. If I need to practice social skills with other people, I will attend a group.
4. Recreation, fun, and social events are important for me and my children. I will set aside time and effort to play.

Feelings for Healthy Parenting
1. I feel good and secure that I can ask for help. I am happy that there are a few people I know I can call on.
2. I feel strong and I feel open to new possibilities when I take charge of my life.
3. I feel pleased that I can look at an area of my life that needs some work and take steps to practice.
4. I have longed to be able to play and have fun with my children and friends. I feel glad to be here with them.

Talking for Healthy Parenting
1. Hello, Joan, how are you doing? You mentioned that I could give you a call if I was in a jam. I am taking this class for parents of hyperactive kids and my babysitter got sick. Would you be able to watch Kevin tonight? (he had his Ritalin already today)
2. It's nice to see you Mary. I was thinking of our conversation

last week about exercise. Would you like to come over Saturday morning and take a power walk with me?

3. Hello, my name is John and I would like to sign up for the family nature walk I saw advertised in the newspaper. Can you give me some information about it?

4. Children, what do you think about having some neighbors and their children over for a potluck dinner? I will need your help to clean up and get ready.

For some single-parents there is an abundance of family, friends and acquaintances to maintain feelings of belonging. In some single-parent families, there is also the other parent who loves and cares for the children. The presence of a father who is involved not only bodes well for the children's development but means that the mother gets some relief time. In any single-family situation where the absent parent maintains a presence and shows concern for the children, those children will fare significantly better in the long run. The children will do even better yet if the ex-spouses can communicate effectively about arrangements and leave off with their own conflicts. Single parents with physical custody of their children help their children a great deal by encouraging visitation and maintaining clear and positive communication with the other parent.

The quality of the communication in families plays a large role in the children's ability to adjust to their home, school, and peers. Families that verbally, emotionally, and physically abuse members are better off apart if they cannot stop the abuse. Hostility and violence are destructive whether children feel it from parents who are married and living together or those who are divorced. Children, who observe healthy communication between their parents, even though they are divorced, will be able to adjust and function in their lives. Even in situations of separation and divorce, studies have clearly demonstrated that parents who communicate clearly and avoid hostility as much as possible produce adjusted children. When the custodial parent makes plans with the other parent in a reasonable manner, the child is free to grow without the threat of fighting and abuse held over her head.

It is not who resides in a child's home that determines the child's mental health and well being rather it is how those adults behave and communicate with each other and with the children. An inevitable scenario in single parent families emerges when the parent begins to have a close relationship with another adult. This scenario is difficult for all involved because each person has needs and wants that may go unmet. Mom meets a man, children resent Mom's time and attention taken away from them and turned toward the man, and Mom feels torn between the man and her children. The man finds it difficult to tolerate needy, dependent, and rejecting children. Get some help with this kind of situation if any one person, child, or adult feels bad. It is important to let an impartial, trained counselor help with feelings and problems that arise when relationships break apart in divorce and then new relationships come together after the divorce.

Given that positive communication is an essential ingredient in family life, let us look deeper into the language style of mothers and fathers to see what is best for children. Is the typical mother's style of talking the same as a typical father's style? Most of us will answer with an emphatic "NO" because we have observed male and female differences in talking to children. We talked about various language styles parents use to teach their children to talk in the first section of this book. We saw that parents simplify their speech by using limited vocabulary, reduced grammatical constructions, clear pronunciation; they slow down the pace of their talk, widen the pitch and use repetition and expansion. Now the fact is that most young children spend more time with their mothers than with their fathers and it is true that mothers tend to simplify their speech more than fathers do.

So even though Mom and Dad have some elements of talk in common, there are differences which impact on the growing child. Mothers, more often than fathers, are likely to talk when they are with babies and children. Moms get talk started with kids and they know how to keep it going. On the other hand, fathers are less likely to understand the sounds and words of their babies and younger children. With older children, Dad may not be familiar with the child's thoughts, wishes, and fantasies. One reason for this is that fathers have spent less time with them and less time talking to them. Another reason that fathers do not understand children as well as mothers is because they are less inclined to go the extra nine yards to figure out what junior said. They hold out a subtle expectation of "Say it right or don't say it." On the other hand, mothers take on an attitude of "I am with you and I'll stick with this comment until I get it."

Fathers use vocabulary more like they would with an adult; they use a wider range of words that are more representative sample of their own vocabulary. Particularly with older children, fathers ask more direct questions that require one specific answer whereas mothers tend to ask for more open-ended responses and accept a wider range of answers. As mentioned, fathers spend less time with children generally and when they are with them their play tends to be more closely interactive and more physical. There may even be more playful teasing, more joking, and more comical routines going with Dad.

When you think about the language roles that mother and father play, it appears as though they are balancing each other's strengths. Mothers are using their language to play a supportive, responsive, sensitive role with their children. Fathers are putting more verbal demands on their children, expecting more independent behavior, and encouraging the child to take on more challenges. Mothers provide a safe haven for expressing feelings and pulling out deep emotions, while fathers push the child to talk in a strong and assertive way.

My understanding of mother's and father's contribution to their child's language development is that of a bird with one left, feminine wing, and one right, masculine wing. The bird cannot fly if one wing is broken; children cannot balance their motivation, thinking, feeling, and talking without the complimentary support

174

of the left and right wings. Neither wing is better, but together they help the child to feel secure, nurtured, and valued while also gaining the confidence and strength to move out into the world.

Both wings are essential for functioning as a mature adult in life; a person must be able to comfort and nurture herself as well as direct and assert herself. When children receive left wing nurture and right wing assertiveness from their parents, they internalize these capacities which become part of their personality. Once part of their personality, these skills of nurture and assertiveness are available at any moment to be called up and utilized. For instance, a child is criticized and she feels hurt and angry. First she must comfort and console herself; in a healthy personality there is a soft inner spot where the mother's voice is present, loving, and reassuring. Then she must decide how to assert herself, how to stand up for herself, and how to say what needs to be said. If these opposite skills of nurture and assertiveness are not present in the child's family life, they will not be present in her personality development.

Single mothers talk to their children with the responsivity and receptivity characteristic of the left wing. Single fathers talk to their children with all the strength and challenge of the right wing. Children need both their left and right wings to fly and, thus, the single parent is motivated to provide some of both masculine and feminine types of verbal support. One way to do this is for single parents to work with an ex-spouse to provide the complementary verbal style through visits and telephone conversations with children. Another way would be to enlist Big Brothers or Big Sisters from legitimate organizations for contact with boys and girls. Awareness of and practice with balancing left and right wings communication is another option. Generally single mothers will practice including assertive talk while fathers will practice nurturing talk. Here are some examples:

SINGLE MOTHER PROVIDING

LEFT AND RIGHT WING COMMUNICATION

Mother: Did you brush your teeth yet? You have to go out to the bus stop in five minutes to catch the school bus.

Daughter: (seven years old) But I don't want to go to school. I have a stomachache. It hurts right around here. (points)

Mother: When did this start? Why didn't you tell me earlier?

Daughter: It did not hurt before. Now it hurts real bad (she is not acting sick and has been chipper all morning).

Mother: Why do you think your stomach is hurting you? Is there something you are worried about?

Daughter: I do not want to go to school. They always want me to go on the tire swing and it makes me feel sick to my stomach.

Mother: Do you think your stomachache has to do with worrying about the tire swing?

Daughter: Maybe, but my stomach does hurt.

Mother: Well, it is hard to tell what is really bothering you right now. I believe that your stomach hurts but I want to find out why it hurts—you could be worried about the tire swing or you could be getting an upset stomach. I feel for you and I know it is not easy to understand all of your aches and pains. But I will talk about it with you and together we can try to figure it out.

Daughter: Thanks Mom. (hugs)

Mother: But for today, I want you to try something new. I want you to go to school and tell your friends you are not going on the tire swing today. Be strong and be the boss of what you do—don't let them tell you what to do.

Daughter: What if they tease me?

Mother: Tease them back.

Daughter: But what if I am still feeling sick?

Mother: I want you to know that if this is flu sickness I will always come and take care of you. To help us find out, you can go to the school nurse and she will be able to help you. She knows more about sickness than I do. Do you think this is a good plan? Do you feel ok?

Daughter: Better.

Mother: Now you better scoot or you will miss the bus.

Mothers tend to stay with their child's feelings and talk until they know what the child feels and why. This is nurturing and supportive to the child. This type of left wing communication helps the child understand her feelings and separate out what problems are physical and what are emotional. In the above example, mom was trying to help her daughter to understand that she could have a stomachache that was from worrying and thinking about the tire swing. In the example, the mother helped her daughter to problem solve which is left wing talk. However she used right wing talk by encouraging her daughter to stand up for herself by saying no to the tire swing pressure. Then she went farther by telling her daughter to tease the other children back if they tease her. This mother knows that children have to be encouraged to stand up for themselves.

From my clinical experience, I believe that children need the nurturing and responsivity that is characteristic of the left wing. They can survive, albeit less well, without the right wing. They will not be able to fly straight without the right wing but I fear they will not be able to fly at all without the left wing. That is why single fathers need to work hard to provide for left wing communication with their children.

SINGLE FATHER PROVIDING
LEFT AND RIGHT WING COMMUNICATION

Father: What's the matter?

Daughter: (comes in from the bus stop crying) Bea and Rick

are always at the bus stop first. They put their bags down in line and then no one else can ever be first on the bus.

Father: Hey, no problem. Let them be first.

Daughter: (crying) But it's not fair. I want to be first sometimes because then I would get to sit in the back seat of the bus and that is the best.

Father: (realizes he has to acknowledge her feelings and her problem) Ok, you are still crying and that means you must be upset. So what do you feel?

Daughter: Really mad! I want you to come out and help me with this. They are bullying me and I am so mad.

Father: Ok, you are so mad that you want me to help. So I will help. What should we do? Let's figure it out before we go out there.

Daughter: I have wanted to be first for a long time now.

Father: Well, you can't be first all the time either, that won't go over well with Bea and Rick. How about if you line up by age, youngest to oldest, and then rotate each morning. The kid who was first today goes to the end of the line the next day while the kid who was second gets to be first and so on.

Daughter: That's great because I am the youngest! I will go first.

Father: Yes, but we have to get everyone to agree first. I'll come out and help work this out. (remembers to show affection) Could I get a hug from you for coming to me and working this out with me?

Daughter: Yeah!

When a man says "No problem" to another man he is indicating that he has confidence in the other man to work out his problems. He is showing that he knows the man can work out his own problems and doesn't need help. This response from a man helps other men to feel competent and capable. But this approach does

178

not work with children, girls nor boys. Children need step by step instructions with lots of empathy and comfort mixed in. In the above example, the father first thought the daughter should go work out the problem herself and then implied she should just give up her feelings about being first. "No problem" does not work with a child in the example given. The father caught himself and back-peddled to acknowledge his daughter's feelings, then help her problem solve. He even remembered a hug at the end.

Alberti, Robert E. and Emmons, Michael, L. Your Perfect Right. Impact Publishers, California, 1992.

Crystal, David Listen To Your Child: A Parents Guide to Children's Language. Penguin Books Ltd, Hammondsworth, Middlesex, England, 1986

Kamerman, Sheila B. & Kahn, Alfred J. Mothers Alone: Strategies for a time of change. Auburn House Publishing Company, Dover Massachusetts, 1988

Key, Mary R. Male/Female Language. The Scarecrow Press, Inc. Metuchen, NJ, 1975.

Mulroy, Elizabeth A. Women As Single Parents: Confronting institutional barriers in the courts, the workplace, and the Housing Market. Auburn House Publishing Company, Westport, Connecticut, 1988.

Victor, Ira & Winkler, Winn Ann   Fathers and Custody Hawthorn Books, Inc. New York, 1977

Chapter 17

Talking and Biking

Becoming a parent is like learning to ride a bicycle. When you are four years old, you watch your eight-year-old sister jump on her bike and pedal off with ease. It looks simple to do and you assume that you can just jump on a bike and ride off also.

Parents-to-be watch parents. They notice how to take care of their children's physical, intellectual, spiritual, and emotional needs. It looks easy to do. People who do not have children assume a person can have a child, like a bike, and automatically jump on and ride.

Of course, neither assumption about riding a bike or parenting is accurate. Both require effort and skill; both are inherently developmental processes.

Step one in riding a bike requires some handling of the bike and some initial shaky attempts to mount it and balance. Initial contact with a bicycle can be humbling for a child as she finds it is heavy, awkward, and high up off the ground. So, step one in riding a bicycle is familiarity with the scope of the task ahead. You must have some idea of what you are going to do.

Likewise in parenting, step one comes when we take our infant home from the hospital. We are alone for the first time with a small human being. We realize we are the sole caretaker and we attempt to take care of the baby. There are no owner's manuals for four-year-old children riding a bike or parents with a newborn. So like the four-year-old with her bike, the new mother and father spend time with their new charge. They learn to handle her, observe her, and figure out how to care for her. Step one recurs for parents at every developmental stage, and, obviously, there are more changes with a growing child than with a bike. Bicycles have training wheels, they come in bigger sizes, they can have gears or hand breaks. With babies, the options are much greater. Each stage of development brings new abilities and new challenges.

Step two in riding a bicycle means sitting on the seat and pushing off for the first time while pumping rapidly on the pedals. The feeling is foreign. How does anyone ever keep this piece of metal upright? Step two is a balanced and brave burst of effort. It is unfamiliar, confusing, demanding, and thrilling. If we remain calm, focused, and keep pedaling we may go several yards before we fall. At times, we need a jump-start so Mom puts on her running shoes.

The parallel to parenting is that we start by talking to our children. We teach them, guide them, and love them the best we can. We have to push off for the first time with the balanced and brave feeling, then stay calm and focused as the needs and twists of childhood unfold. We usually can go for sometime before we fall off. When we fall off our parenting bike, we meet up with a problem such as illness or some unwanted behavior that causes us to stop and reevaluate. Then we must problem solve which eventually gets us back on the parenting bike again.

Step three in learning to ride a bike comes when Susie has courageously pushed off a hundred times, pedaled hard, and found her balance. She knows she can stay up for at least a short time. She is on her wheels and can stay up as long as she does not have to turn or navigate obstacles. Now she can concentrate on the subtleties of biking. She can experiment with speed, direction, turning, bell ringing, or whatever else she wants.

181

Mom and Dad go through step three when they begin to feel confident about their ability to adapt to the rhythm of the child's needs and formulate a philosophy of parenting that works for them. Step three is the longest step and it is epitomized by subtle refinement of skills and sensitivity.

After reading through this book and understanding more about the nature of parent-child relationships, parents are prepared for more successful interactions and conversations with children. Parents will have good reason to feel hopeful that they can reach their children through communication and keep the talk going.

I have seen many parents transform their relationships with their children into much deeper and more rewarding family patterns using the ideas laid out here. By remembering to talk to children with openness, tenderness, and acceptance you can have success as a parent.

Parents can focus on the three steps of bike parenting. Before step one it looks easy but know that looks are deceiving. There is nothing easy about jumping on a metal device and thrusting yourself forward against gravity. Parenting is hard, gentle work, and requires courage to keep learning and stay open to changes with each stage.

Step two in parenting lasts a long time and overlaps with step three. We have to keep getting up on the bike and opening ourselves to bumps and turns and cars passing by. As parents we need to listen to our heart and good advice; the combination of which makes for a bumpy ride. How do we blend our needs, our inner voice with what we hear from other parents and professionals?

In step three we may feel discouraged at times because even though we have been riding smoothly for a while, we can expect bumps and detours. We may blame ourselves when problems arise and start to feel helpless, empty, and doubtful. This is all part of the bike-parenting cycle. Children's problems and family troubles are a necessary part of life and what helps during these times is to stay in step three. Focus, balance, keep pedaling and you will be open to new learning, insights, and the subtleties of communication.

Sometimes talk flows easily and automatically. Sometimes our hearts are overflowing with love and empathy for our children. At times, we have endless patience and understanding. And then it all begins to give way and frustration and impatience mount. We cannot expect ourselves to be open, receptive, and capable of listening and processing with our children at all times. A "Quiet Time" request can be used whenever it is needed. Rocky roads and frost heaves make biking tough at times and that is ok. We must not expect ourselves to be perfect or perfectly understanding.

In Step three of biking you will inevitably take a wrong turn. When you are on a bike you can get lost and get confused about which way to turn. Expect to take many wrong turns in parenting; all parents do. It is impossible to navigate such a complicated vehicle throughout such rough terrain without a few breakdowns and wrong turns. Talk about the wrong turns; make them part of regular family discussion. Talk openly about parent mistakes and acknowledge how hard a job it is. And ultimately get to the point of being able to laugh about the wrong turns after the strong feelings have passed.

By talking to children with firmness, love, and compassion parents can get the close relationships they want, need, and deserve. Even if Moms and Dads don't remember anything else from this book, they will remember to talk to their children and let them talk. If parents can do this, they have a great deal of intimacy and happiness to look forward to.

Help Is But A Click Away -

A MESSAGE FROM THE PUBLISHER

In my troubled youth, I discovered the hope and knowledge available in self-help books. Reading such books helped me so much and eventually was instrumental in my becoming a psychologist. I subsequently went on to write five self-help books and spent 25 years investigating how such books help people cope with life's problems. I was so impressed by the power of self-help books that when the Internet became so prevalent in our lives, I quickly realized it was the ideal place where people could find the right self-help book for their particular problem. *SelfHelpBooks.com* emerged and is my way of making good self-help easily available to anyone who is distressed and in need of help.

SelfHelpBooks.com publishes books by mental health professionals as well as by lay people who have coped well with life's adversity and have some valuable advice to pass on to the rest of us. The many titles that can be found in *SelfHelpBooks.com*'s virtual bookstore have been carefully selected to provide help for a range of problems from addiction to depression, from phobic fear to loneliness, and from problems of youth to problems of the elderly.

You may not find the proverbial rose garden, but you can learn how to start smelling the roses. At *SelfHelpBooks.com* we think we have a book for almost every problem. With just three mouse clicks you should be able to find a book to suit your needs. If you need help immediately, you can download it as an E book. If you are in less of a hurry, you can order a print version and receive it within days.

If you visit SelfHelpBooks.com and don't find a book relating to your particular problem, contact us and we will immediately add several books in that category. If you know of a particular good self-help book that has helped you, let us know and we will add it to our list.

Harold H. Dawley, Jr., Ph.D., ABPP
Publisher

Printed in the United States
2515